The Best Women's Stage Monologues of 1992

Jocelyn A. Beard has edited

The Best Men's Stage Monologues of 1990,

The Best Women's Stage Monologues of 1990,

The Best Men's Stage Monologues of 1991,

The Best Women's Stage Monologues of 1991,

One Hundred Men's Stage Monologues from the 1980's,

One Hundred Women's Stage Monologues from the 1980's,

and has co-edited

The Best Stage Scenes for Men from the 1980's

and The Best Stage Scenes for Women from the 1980's.

Other Books for Actors from Smith and Kraus

MONOLOGUES

The Best Men's Stage Monologues of 1992
The Best Men's Stage Monologues of 1991
The Best Men's Stage Monologues of 1990
The Best Women's Stage Monologues of 1992
The Best Women's Stage Monologues of 1991
The Best Women's Stage Monologues of 1990
Street Talk: Character Monologues for Actors
One Hundred Men's Stage Monologues from the 1980's
One Hundred Women's Stage Monologues from the 1980's
The Great Monologues from the Humana Festival
The Great Monologues from the EST Marathon
Monologues from Contemporary Literature: Volume I
Monologues from Classic Plays
Uptown: Character Monologues for Actors

YOUNG ACTORS

Great Scenes for Young Actors from the Stage
Great Monologues for Young Actors
New Plays from A.C.T.'s Young Conservatory
Scenes and Monologues for Very Young Actors

ADVANCED ACTORS

The Best Stage Scenes for Women from the 1980's
The Best Stage Scenes for Men from the 1980's
The Best Stage Scenes of 1992
The Actor's Chekhov

PLAYS FOR ACTORS

The Best Plays of 1992 by Women Playwrights
Seventeen Short Plays by Romulus Linney

If you require pre-publication information about upcoming Smith and Kraus
monologues collections, scene collections, play anthologies, advanced acting
books, and books for young actors, you may receive our semi-annual
catalogue, free of charge, by sending your name and address to Smith and
Kraus Catalogue, P.O. Box 10, Newbury, VT 05051.

The Best Women's Stage Monologues of 1992

Edited by
Jocelyn A. Beard

The Monologue Audition Series

SK
A Smith and Kraus Book

A Smith and Kraus Book
Published by Smith and Kraus, Inc.

Copyright © 1992 by Smith and Kraus, Inc.
All rights reserved

Cover and text Design by Julia Hill
Manufactured in the United States of America

First Edition: January 1993
10 9 8 7 6 5 4 3 2 1

Publisher's Cataloging in Publication
(Prepared by Quality Books Inc.)

The Best women's stage monologues of 1992 / edited by Jocelyn A. Beard. - 1st ed.
    p. cm.
Includes bibliographical references.
ISBN 1-880399-10-5

1. Acting. 2. Monologues. I. Beard, Jocelyn A. II. Title:
Best women's stage monologues of nineteen ninety-two.

PN2080.B4 1993a   792'.028
                                         QBI92-2795

Smith and Kraus, Inc.
Main Street, P.O. Box 10, Newbury, Vermont 05051
(802) 866 5423

Acknowledgments

Grateful thanks

to the playwrights and their agents.

Jocelyn A. Beard

would also like to thank

Kevin Kitowski

for his love and support.

TABLE OF CONTENTS

vii

Foreword

What a season! With shows like *Dancing at Lughnasa, Spike Heels* and *Criminal Hearts* gracing our stages this year, it's no wonder that our annual collection of monologue material is brimming with wonderful selections for women. In a year that the feminist movement found itself put to the test, it is particularly inspiring that women's roles in theatre have continued to evolve without hindrance from the socio-political factors found daily in our national op-ed pages.

The women of the 1992 theatrical season can be found struggling in Ireland in the 1930's, hiding in a township in strife-ridden South Africa and in, perhaps, the most dangerous of all locations: the dreaded Fire Island vacation home in Terrence McNally's *Lips Together Teeth Apart*. Tackling life's challenges with breathtaking courage and passion, the women found withing these pages point us towards the future.

Playwrights like Joyce Carol Oates and John Patrick Shanley have created women's characters in 1992 that enchant, educate and provoke. 1992 gives us women fighting to take back their lives, women facing the inevitability of disease and death, women coping with the destruction of their country and women struggling to claim their birthright. Happily, all is not dire. Plenty of comedic and downright silly characters have been included in the collection, rounding it out in a delightful manner.

Hopefully, you will find several pieces herein that will round out your own collection.

Break a leg!

Jocelyn A. Beard
Patterson, NY
Autumn 1992

Introduction

I have always felt that an actor could probably call themselves truly professional when they were able to do three things well; get enough work in their chosen field, to feel that they were indeed supplementing their acting work by being a waiter or waitress and not the other way around, handle the inevitable rejection that comes their way at least 90% of the time, and, finally, actually begin to enjoy the audition process.

I know that, as a director, I enjoy auditions. I love reading actors for a specific part in a particular play. I find that I learn so much about the material by watching the different ways people interpret it, and often feel that I should thank all the people I didn't cast for teaching me a lot about the play as well as all the people I did cast when opening night rolls around. I even like the dreaded general audition. I enjoy seeing what plays and monologues people choose to introduce themselves.

I hope that all of you reading this book can look at the audition process in this positive way. It should be fun. It should be interesting for you to choose a piece, and, when the actual audition comes, it should be interesting for you to assess how well you were actually able to perform that piece. The monologues contained in this volume give you many good choices. And that is, after all, what the general audition, the sort of audition you will be most likely about to attend if you are looking through this book, is all about-showing the director as much as you can about your ability to make choices.

The first choice you will make will be the piece itself. Choose a piece that really moves you and can sustain your own interest as you spend time getting it ready for your audience. Then make wise choices about presentation. Stay close to your own instincts and your own level of technical proficiency. Remember, this is just an introduction. As your audience, I'll be looking for very simple things with this audition. I'm hoping that the piece you will have chosen will be something new for me (and this volume will give you plenty of ideas for monologues that aren't being used by almost every other actor,) and that the choices you make as you deliver the piece reveal your intelligence and humanity.

Allow these monologues to take you to other places. Read the whole play if you like the monologue. Read other works by the same author. Most of all, enjoy the process. No matter what comes of the audition, the process itself will have its own rewards.

Sharon Ott
Artistic Director
Berkely Repertory Theatre

The Best Women's Stage Monologues of 1992

ANOTHER TIME
by Ronald Harwood
Cape Town, South Africa, (50's)
Rose, a well-meaning Aunt, 51 years old

Rose's nephew is a gifted pianist and has been told by his teacher that he should study in Vienna or New York. Here, Rose insists that he study in London.

ROSE: Leonard, I knew this day would come. I've thought about it often. I want you to develop not only into a great musician but also into a great artist. I want you to use London, I want you to-I argue it this way. London's the only place for you. London is the centre of the world. The most cultured people on earth gravitate towards London. They have the finest theatres in the world, the finest libraries. They have art galleries and concert halls. They have Winston Chruchill and that gorgeous Anthony Eden. They have the finest system of government in the world. Did you know, Leonard, that in England when a Cabinet Minister leaves the presence of the King he has to walk backwards? Please God he should trip. And those two little darlings, Elizabeth and Margaret Rose. We are talking about a city, about Mecca, about Jerusalem, about London, about England. But you know above all what England has? England has English. Now, this is a language. Imagine, Leonard, if there'd been no pogroms. You know what you'd be talking now? Lithuanian. This is not a language. English is a language. And thank God for the Empire. Without the British Empire you'd be talking Zulu. How could you go to Vienna? What sort of language is German? It's a language for shouting orders. But English. Oh, Leonard, what a language. Take time to read, I beg you. Music may be your life, Leonard, but, believe me, without books a person may as well be dead. You can keep your Russians, your Dostoevsky and Tolstoy, you can keep your French-Zola and Flaubert are good only for insomnia. But, for life, Leonard, as I always tell anyone who cares to listen, for life, Leonard, devour William Shakespeare, drink John Milton, taste Jane Austen, consume George Eliot, drown in Charles Dickens, glory in John Donne, whisper Wordsworth when you walk, befriend Robert Browning and let William Blake invade your dreams and nightmares. And if you are blue, I know you'll listen to the music that inspires you, but

1

do me this favor, reach out for P.G. Wodehouse. Never mind he was a German spy, genius and decency don't always walk hand in hand-look at Wagner-but P.G. Wodehouse writes English to make Thomas Mann illiterate. I thank God that your mother, your Uncle Zodok and I were born in London. It's given us-it's given us culture. New York. Please. Americans are about as cultured as Miss Anna Katz. Have you read this man, Mailer?

[LEONARD: No-]

ROSE: Don't read him, Leonard, with his fug and fugging. Filth. But that's America. Norman Mailer. And to what American did they award a Nobel Prize for Literature? Pearl S. Buck, that's all they could find. Pearl S. Buck, I ask you. Mind you, she makes even Norman Mailer look as if he can write. No, No, Leonard. English. England. London. I want you to promise me you'll read, Leonard, you'll go to theatres and art galleries-and remember, always wear a tie when you go into the centre of London. It's the respect you pay a great city. And one more thing. How would you have managed in Vienna? At your school they don't teach languages, they teach Afrikaans. Afrikaans. Pearl S. Buck should have written in Afrikaans, it may have improved her style.

ANOTHER TIME
by Ronald Harwood
Cape Town, South Africa, (50's)
Belle, a woman coping with her husband's death, 40's

When her husband dies suddenly, Belle vows to make a better
future for her son and herself.

BELLE: Doctors. What do they know? Meningioma. Sounds
like something a poet should die from. Meningioma. Shall I
read what David Figg says? A G.P.A. top man. *(She Picks up a
letter. Reading.)* "Meningioma means a tumor growning along
the blood vessels on the surface of the brain. It can be either
malignant or benign. In your late husband's case, the tumor was
benign. We know very little about such growths. The
pathologist is of the opinion that the tumor had been present for
several years but that its development was erratic. For long
periods it would, apparently, lie dormant and then, due perhaps
to some emotional or physical disturbance, become active,
causing slow progressive damage to the brain. What is puzzling
is that Mr. Lands did not suffer unduly from the symptoms one
would normally expect, such as severe headaches or convulsive
seizures. I hope all of this is of some help. I wish you and your
son long life. David Figg." *(Silence.)*

Meningioma. And David Figg was the doctor who said mind
over matter. Doctors. What do they know? *(Silence.)*

You know the worst two words in the English language,
Leonard, in any language? "If only." *(Silence.)*

It makes me laugh. Everything these days is psychology.
Everybody's blaming their parents or their nannies, everybody's
suffering from an unhappy childhood or some shock to their
system they can't talk about until Freud interprets their dreams
and life is suddenly bearable again Everybody's haunted by
their own past. Trust Ike to be different. With Ike it was never
just one thing. With him it couldn't just be mind over matter, it
couldn't just be a growth on the brain, it had to be both. Such a
complex man. Meningioma. "If only." *(Silence.)*

Leonard, I wish you'd cry. I'm stifled with foreboding.

3

(Silence.)

I should have known he was seriously ill when he mentioned the shadows under my eyes. Twenty-five years of marriage and the first time he says anything about my eyes is on the day he dies. *(Silence.)*

I'm not going to be haunted. I'm not going to ruin the rest of my life with guilt. I'm not going to apologize. We fought. We argued. I'm a difficult woman. He was a difficult man. I'm not going to lie. We only fought about one thing. Perhaps money was a symbol, who knows? *(Silence.)*

I can't weep either. But that's all right. I've seen those widows at their husbands' funerals, they throw themselves into the grave, weep and wail and tear their hair out. They're always the quickest to remarry. *(Silence.)*

I'm never going to lie about Ike and me. I won't bathe his memory in sunshine. *(Silence.)*

The past is the past. What will be, will be. I'm a fatalist. We have to make plans, Leonard. We have to think only of the future, your future. You'll go overseas, Vienna, London, New York, wherever. Don't worry, somehow you'll go. If I have to eat one meal a week, you'll go. I'll work to the end of the chapter. As long as there's a purpose I don't mind. Because, to tell you the truth, Leonard, there's nothing else I care about except your future. Not now. I always thought when I had you that I couln't be alone ever again. Well, one can always be wrong. I have total confidence in you, I believe in your gifts, I have absolute faith. You're my future, Leonard. The past can go to hell. *(Silence. Lights fade to Blackout.)*

4

APPOINTMENT WITH A HIGH WIRE LADY
by Russell Davis
A psychiatric center, Present
Louise, 20's

Louise speaks to her ex-boyfriend Richard who is confined in a catatonic state.

LOUISE: I'm sorry. I seem angry. Probably hurt. I shouldn't feel at all hurt. Considering what's happened to you. But I think it upsets me, screws me up, because I think I told you long ago this could happen. I knew deep down long ago you weren't interested. That there was something in you that was simply not interested in living past a certain point in your life. And therefore that's how you behaved. As if you weren't going to be around after a certain point. And it makes me, a little bit mad, because it attracted me so much, and it screwed me up so much, and I think it was the hardest thing I ever had to do was to get out of the way of how you weren't going to be around after a certain point. And I did. I got out of the way. And it feels terrible now. It feels years later you stepped off a building or something. You finally let certain things lapse. Because it's exactly like you fell off some terrible height, and you didn't intend this, I'm sure you didn't, but you've landed. And probably you'll never again ever be anything like what you used to be. (*Pause.*) And I think that's a terrible thing to give to the people you know. (*Pause.*) Or used to know.

ASCENSION DAY
by *Michael Henry Brown*
Virginia, 1831
Cherry, the wife of Nat Turner, African-American, 20's

Cherry has been raped by Master Reese, the plantation owner.
Here, she bitterly tells her tragic story to her husband.

CHERRY: Massa Reese come in my shack las' night. *(Pause.)*
He be real nice. Tell me not to worry 'bout Briley since I wit
chile an' all. Den...he begin to take his clothers off...an' he
crawl up beside me... *(Long Pause.)* De babies be still awake.
I starts to beg him nots to do dis, an' he tells me dat when he
ride his horse it don't give him no back talk, an' so when he ride
me he don't 'spect non neither. *(Pause.)* An' while he be
humpin' me, an' a slobberin' all ovah me...I looks ovah an' sees
Redic tryin' ta cover Daisy's eyes...an' she be lettin' out a flood
o' tears...But Redic, he be a starin' at us wit death in his eyes.
An' Massa Stay dere all night...humpin'me...An' Redic ain't
sleep he jest watch. Don't 'spect him ta evah sleep peaceful like
again. *(Pause.)* Don't 'spect I evah will either.

THE BABY
by Chris Hannan
Rome, a shrine in a wood, 78 BC
Ranee, a healer, 30-60

During the bloody riots of 78 BC, a healer enjoys a peaceful moment in a shrine.

RANEE: You'll have heard the news by now I take it. Sulla got his funeral. - The man with the pus-sy eye that works in the women's baths and scalded my belly that time with the boiling jug of water for no earthly reason that I could see except that he's a bad bastard: he told me. Then he gave me one of his smirks. Only he's got an infection of the mouth just now so he just looked stupid. I said to him, what's wrong with your mouth, is that thrush you've got? - I was right too. - Now Lepidus has raised an army up north, he's marching on Rome; only, Pompey has raised another army up north and he's marching on Lepidus. They say Lepidus is seven days ahead. - Thank you for the day. More people came to me today, to be healed. Two of them had nothing wrong with them so that was easy enough. Then there was the two who had devils in them. Then a woman who had burned her hands and couldn't hold things. So I healed her and cast out the two devils then I went to the baths. - I love woods. Even in spring, dead leaves: soft, think rot. And the quiet. Like the whole wood is listening. When a bird sings you can hear every note...the pauses. One day I'll come here, bury myself under the dead leaves and die. - They say all kinds of rubbish, they don't even listen to it themselves. I come and pray in secret because you live in secret, like the healing plants, you wait for me. - I saw the Vetch today. There's a god and a half: big, and stupid with it. He'd a big shaggy tree over his shoulder, he'd pulled it out of the ground like a vegetable, roots and all and he was off to plant it somewhere else. He likes that. He moves a tree from one part of the wood to another then the next day he moves it back again. - I'll go now. - Oh, the two devils. One was called Hista and one was called Geb. I drove them into some black rocks. (*Exits.*)

BEGGARS IN THE HOUSE OF PLENTY
by John Patrick Shanley
A dusty basement of a home in the Bronx
Ma, a loveless matriarch, 45-60

When her adult son turns to her for love, Ma bitterly rejects his overtures.

MA: I spotted you right off. When you'd grunt at me, look me in the eye, shit yourself so satisfied. When you'd waddle around the rug like an old lecher with his belly and his craven face: "What's for me?" You did everything with an eye to how I'd take it. Everything was a test. In the tub you'd look at me, and your pecker'd pop up, and you'd smile! It was like the Devil smirkin in my face! I became afflicted by these awful headaches and horrible dreams of blood and mayhem. But I had your number! I knew you thought only about your functions and your pecker, and I just tried not to look you in the eye cause then you'd give me that big dirty stare. Looking into me. Trying to get at me. Big eyes! I'm not your guinea pig! And then, when you realized that I wouldn't look at you, you wouldn't look at me, and that I found out was dangerous, too! You started doing things. Playing with matches, hiding things, breaking things, stealing things, lying about it all. Mischief! Mischief! I thought I'd go mad!

BLACK FRIDAYS?
by Audrey Butler
A living room in Cape Breton, Canada, the Present
Spike, a dyke philosopher, 20's

Here, a woman of great confidence explains herself to her lover's ex.

SPIKE: I'm a dyke -

[**RODDY:** Yeah -]

SPIKE: A virtual dykology.
I been a bar dyke.
A dude dyke.
A birkenstock dyke.
Now I'm a bike dyke.

[**RODDY:** Why do you have to be so blatant about it?]

SPIKE: Why not? Better blatant than latent.
Two women fucking may be just a turn-on for some men
but for some lesbians it means taking our own pleasure
in our own hands and coming a lot

[**RODDY:** It's just the sex? C'mon.]

SPIKE: Oh, Roddy, it's everything -
it's the way they walk, the way they talk-
the way they think.
Their stories.
Their hands. Their hearts. Their loving wise ways.
The way they make me feel.
So-o-o-o-o good.
When I was little I didn't know what a "girl" was -
I didn't know I was a girl -
Not a "boy," but not a girl either.
I was just me. A "tweensy."

(Roddy laughs, understanding.)

9

Now I feel like a whole person.
Naw, fucking is only part of it, Roddy.
The idea of women having sex in a society -
that hates sex,
and women, not to mention lesbians -
makes it dangerous.
For me. For us.
I hate the danger, but I take it on.
Because I'm a dyke.
I love women.
Does that answer your question?

BOLD GIRLS
by Rona Munro
A flat in Belfast, Northern Ireland, the Present
Marie, a young woman trying to
hold onto life in war-torn Belfast, 30's

The violence in Northern ireland has claimed the life of Marie's
husband, Michael. Here, she recalls the day they were married.

MARIE: It was a terrible wet day when I got married. A wet
grey day in 1974 and I couldn't get to the church for the road
blocks. I was standing out on my step there with my Mummy
screaming at me to come before I got my good white dress dirty
from the rain...only I was wetter from crying than the clouds
could make me, because Michael Donnelly was the only boy I'd
ever wanted for myself and me just seventeen. He was the only
boy I'd wanted at all and it was still a miracle to me he wanted
me back...but then since I've always had to work hardest at
believing miracles and anyway I knew they only fell in the laps
of the pure in heart, not it seemed certain to me that a pile of
Brits and a road block would lose me Michael altogether...for
why would he wait an hour or more at the church, when he'd
that smile on him that made you feel wicked and glad about it
and that look to him that caught your eye when he was walking
down the street. Just with the way he put his feet down, bold
and happy together, and those hands that were so warm and
gentle you hardly worried where he was putting them and why
would a man like that wait two hours in a cold church for a wee
girl in a damp wedding dress?

And my Mummy's trying to pull my Daddy in 'cause he's
shouting at the Brits saying this was the greatest day of his
daughter's life and hadn't they just spoiled it altogheter? Then
this big Saracen's pulled up and thy've all jumped out and my
Mummy's just going to scream when do they not offer us an
escort throught the road block? So that was my bridal car to the
wedding, a big Saracen full of Brits all grinning and offering us
fags and pleased as punch with themselves for the favour they
were doing us. I hardly dared look at them. I was certain the
big hulk sitting next to me was one of them that had lifted
Michael just the year before but oh they were nice as anything.

11

There was wanted men at the wedding and everything. Sure I'd grey hairs before I was ever married.

And then I was married and Michael brought me here and the rain stopped; it even looked like the sun had come out and I stared and stared, just standing at the top of the path in my wee white dress that was still half soaked. It felt like we'd won through everything, the weather and the road blocks and the Brits and there were never going to be bad times again...because I was never going to be without him again.

Well...I was just seventeen after all.

BOLD GIRLS
by Rona Munro
A flat in Belfast, Northern Ireland, the Present
Marie, a young woman trying to
hold onto life in war-torn Belfast, 30's

As she tidies the kitchen, Marie muses on the unhappy fates of all
the men in her life.

MARIE: I like the pigeons. I saw a pigeon fly across the sky
and when it crossed the clouds it was black but when it flew past
the roofs it was white. It could fly as far as it liked but it never
went further than Turf Lodge from what I could see.

I used to watch for that bird, the only white bird that wasn't a
seagull.

He wasn't even the man they wanted, but they shot him; that
made him the man they wanted.

You have to imagine the four of them. All men you'd look at
twice one way or another. Michael, my husband, because he
had that strong feel to him. You felt it in the back of your neck
when he came in a room. People truned to look without
knowing why. Davey, my brother now, you'd look again but
you'd say, what's that wee boy doing in his Daddy's jacket.
Nineteen and he looks more like nine, though they've put age in
his eyes for him now. He's got old eyes now. Martin, Cassie's
brother, you'd look and you'd cross the street in case he caught
your eye and decided he didn't like the look of you. He's got
the kind of eyebrows that chop short conversations, slamming a
glower on his face like two fists hitting a table...and Joe, Cassie's
husband. You'd look at him to see what the joke was, Joe's
always laughing, Joe's always where the crack is.

Davey's in the Kesh. Martin's in the Kesh. Joe's in the Kesh and
Michael is dead.

They didn't really go round together, the four of them, just
every odd Saturday they'd be in here playing cards till they
were three of them broke and Joe stuffed with beer and
winnings. Singing till they were too drunk to remember the

13

words then waking and eating and drinking some more till they were drunk enought to make up their own. Sure it was a party they had. And Davey felt like a man and Martin smiled and Joe sang almost in tune and Michael would tell me he loved me over and over till he'd make a song out of that.

Sometimes he said he loved me when he'd no drink in him at all. Sometimes he even did that.

(Marie finished tidying, exits.)

BUBBLING
by *Le Wilhelm*
A curio shop in Missouri, the Present
Zoe Ann, a woman trying to recapture her past, 30-40

When a domestic altercation prompts Zoe Ann to pay a visit to her old friend, Julie, the two women find themselves smoking pot and remembering days gone by. Here, Zoe Ann recalls a drug-induced experience with mytho-poetic overtones.

ZOE ANN: You remember that black club that used to be out north of town?

[**JULIE:** BeBops.]

ZOE ANN: John and I were going there to dance, and we took some of the stuff. We got there, and police cars were all over the place, red lights swirling, sirens--and I'm coming on. Oh, Lord, I was scared. I was driving that old blue Ford.

[**JULIE:** *(Smiling)* What else?]

ZOE ANN: And I just kept driving on down the road. Didn't know where the hell I was going. Just knew I wasn't going to BeBops. John said we ought to go to the river. The river that was back the other way. So somehow I got turned around, and we started back. I was so stoned I couldn't tell how fast I was driving. I just kept an eye on the speedometer and hoped it was right. And John's not saying nothing, and I look over, and John's just staring straight ahead, and then I look closer, and he's a goddamn skeleton. And I say, "John," and he says, "Yeah?" And I know it's alright, cause skeletons can't talk. I roll down the window so I can feel the air, and I feel the wind blow right through me. Honest to God, I could feel the wind blowing right through me. I'm driving down Highway 65 at 55, and I'm sitting next to a skeleton, and the wind is blowing through me. *(Looking at Julie)* You've heard this story before, haven't you?

[**JULIE:** Uh huh.]

ZOE ANN: But not all of it. Part of it I've never told anyone.

15

[**JULIE:** Go on.]

ZOE ANN: Finally, we get to the river. And the river's so peaceful, and there's a place on the other side where there's willows and a sand bar and, of course, that's where I want to be. Only problem is it's on the other side of the river. And you know what I did? I walked across the water. I'm not shitting you. I walked across the fucking water. John says he saw me and that he walked on water, too. And so we get to the sand bar, and we just sit there in the moonlight. And then for some reason, I start thinking about dying. Not suicide. Just leaving, going away to rest in the bosom of Abraham. And then I start thinking about all my friends and how I don't want to leave them. But you know, Julie, I always will think that I could have. I could have just left this body and gone away. Gone.

[**JULIE:** But you didn't.]

ZOE ANN: [No,] I didn't. I stayed and let John fuck me.

CRIMINAL HEARTS
by Jane Martin
An expensive condo in Chicago, the Present
Ata, a romantic agoraphobic, 30's

Ata's husband has left her with nothing more than the clothes on her back and a mattress to sleep on. When her condo is broken into, the commotion alerts her neighbor. Here, Ata does her best to assure her neighbor that all is well.

ATA: I'm all right, Ms. Carnahan. Really, I'm all right. I'm not in any danger, no danger of any kind. I'm not harmed or threatened or in trouble. But, the thing is, Mrs. Carnahan, I'm not going to open the door because there's no need and the other reason is...I'm with a lover, Mrs. Carnahan, a lover, a beautiful man who makes my life worth living, who gives meaning to my existence and the thing is, you see, that we are without clothes, that's the thing, we are scented and oiled and pomaded and fresh from the act of love, and so to open the door would be a betrayal for us and an embarrassment for you and then we would feel judged, you see, and the spell, the spell would be broken, because having lived the life you have, you know how fragile these things are. And after our pleasantries, after you were satisfied with my condition and had gone back to your rooms, my lover, the spell broken, would dress and kiss me somewhat impersonally and close the door behind him with the faintest click, Mrs. Carnahan, and I would be alone, at a time when being alone feels...well, feels very worrisome because other things that give meaning...well, they get harder and harder to come by, don't they, Mrs. Carnahan? *(The lights beginning to fade)* Harder and harder to go out and meet these things which seem more and more without meaning and feeling more and more alone and feeling more and more as if that is perfectly all right, that it's very compelling to be alone without meaning when that's probably the worst idea really. So I won't be opening the door, Mrs. Carnahan, because I don't want to end up alone in here and liking it. *(It is down to a single spotlight)* I really don't. I really don't. I really don't. *(The light is out)*

17

CRIMINAL HEARTS
by Jane Martin
An expensive condo in Chicago, the Present
Ata, a romantic agoraphobic, 30's

Here, Ata unleashes years of stored-up angst as she confronts her
insensitive husband with his inadequacies.

ATA: *(Wildly and passionately)* Because I an not...I am not,
not, not, not sorry, because to be sorry would be madness, and I
am not sorry. I am, I'll tell you what I am, I am bemused at
what has happened to me because I signified at one time, I was
redolent with promise, fecund with promise, and now I am
bleached like a cow skull in a Georgia O'Keefe painting. And
what is the sun I curled up under? The radiance I melted away
in? Why it's you, Wib. Under your influence I sharpen pencils
and eat pepperoni pizza, confined in an empty space with my
Dr. Pepper. I am the victim of evaporation of moral fluids, and
you are the drought. You are smug and conventional with your
place assured and your habits ingrained. You are a second-rate
lawyer in a corrupt system doing unimportant paperwork for
the scum of the corporate ear in a salmon and green office in an
architecturally insignificant skyscraper in the midst of an urban
sprawl six blocks from your pre-fab condo that you got a brain-
dead interior designer to fill with mail-order furniture that
thousands of other second-rate lawyers have dignified with their
purchases and mistaken for something they liked. Your
conversations is a rehash of magazines you subscirbe to,
newspapers you read and television you watch without a single
self-generated idea or actual concern you didn't co-opt from
whatever conservatively correct positions you have self-
consciously adopted. You have no passions, or politics, or pain,
or paradise; you have golf clubs. The books you don't read are
the seminal works of the century, and the books you do read are
the junk mail of publishing. You can't fix your car or your
toilet, you can't make anything, build anything, or change
anything. You've never eaten something you caught or killed
or grew or cooked other than to throw it on a barbecue and
make sure it's rare. You have no sense of the transcendental or
the mystical, or the spiritual, you don't even have a cookie-cutter
religion to give you something to do on Sunday, other than the
Chicago Tribune. You never fought in a war or lost a child or

18

lost anything except your car keys and your glasses and your temper and your credit cards. You don't have a coherent family or a community you love, or close friends, or even a pet, a dog, a cat, or a parakeet; you have a car phone. Your idea of love is getting it up, and getting it up is all you think about when you make love so that nobody gets anything back from you even when you're inside them because you are in a new kind of super-hero, you are scarecrow man got up for a power lunch and completely devoid of a center or a soul or a commitment except to keep the birdshit off your shoulders with a smile painted on your face as you scare everything alive out of its wits with this phoney intimidation that wouldn't even kill or maim because it's just another function of any empty vessel wich is all you are, Wib, you are the Flying Dutchman of the 90's, plowing right along, wind in the sails, pretty as a picture, and nobody, *nobody* at the wheel! So I am going out, far out, way out, out beyond you, because I need to see what few real things I can get inside me before it's too late, and there is no way to get them from you, because the lights are on at your house but there's nobody home!

DANCING AT LUGHNASA
by Brian Friel
The Home of the Mundy family,
Ballybeg, County Donegal,Ireland, 1936
Maggie, a housekeeper, 38

When her sister tells her that she saw an old childhood friend in
the village, Maggie remembers a happier time in the past.

MAGGIE: When I was sixteen I remember slipping out one
Sunday night - it was this time of year, the beginning of August
-and Bernie and I met at the gate of the workhouse and the pair
of us off to a dance in Ardstraw. I was being pestered by a
fellow called Tim Carlin at the time but it was really Brian
McGuinness that I was - that I was keen on. Remember Brian
with the white hands and the longest eyelashes you ever saw?
But of course he was crazy about Bernie. Anyhow the two boys
took us on the bar of their bikes and off the four of headed to
Ardstraw, fifteen miles each way. If Daddy had known, may he
rest in peace...

And at the end of the night there was a competition for the Best
Military Two-step. And it was down to three couples: the local
pair from Ardstraw; wee Timmy and myself - he was up to there
on me; and Brian and Bernie...

And they were just so beautiful together, so stylish; you couldn't
take your eyes off them. People just stopped dancing and
gazed at them...

And when the judges announced the winners - they were
probably blind drunk - naturally the local couple came first;
and Timmy and myself came second; and Brian and Bernie
came third.

Poor Bernie was stunned. She couldn't believe it. Couldn't talk.
Wouldn't speak to any of us for the rest of the night. Wouldn't
even cycle home with us. She was right, too: they should have
won; they were just so beautiful together...And that's the last
time I saw Brian McGuinness - remember Brian with the...?
And the next thing I heard he had left for Australia...

20

She was right to be angry, Bernie. I know it wasn't fair - it wasn't fair at all. I mean they must have been blind drunk, those judges, whoever they were...

DARK SUN
by Lisette Lecat Ross
A house in the poorer section
of Soweto, South Africa, 1988
Lydia De Jager, a white South African
struggling to comprehend her country's problems, 30-40

Lydia organizes Red Cross bus tours of Soweto. She alone survives a violent attack on a bus thanks to the heroic efforts of Simon, a resident of the township, who risks all to hide her in his house while a riot continues to rage outside. Pretending to be a member of the Red Cross, Lydia here describes the attack.

LYDIA: It was all so quick. You know. Somehow we got further and further into this area, I dunno how, he'd done it - I mean, he must have done it a thousand times before. He was black, he must have known the area. Just as I began to think, this is definitely wrong - I was going to tell him, when the bomb went off. It was just terrible. *(Begins to relive it.)* It exploded right in front of the bus. The only person hurt was the driver - from the glass and stuff. But it could have been me, I was right behind him. There was blood all over him. I don't think he knew what he was doing because that's when the bus crashed into the wall. Everyone was screaming. He jumped out and he started running like crazy. That's when they threw the other bomb - a grenade or something - it went off outside but it broke some bus windows. Glass went everywhere. People started pushing and shouting. Everyone trying to get out. It was awful. Then the crowds. Blacks. Came from everywhere. There were a lot of young men - boys really - shouting and cheering and jumping up and down. *(Voice cracks.)* Hugging each other. Nobody knew what to do. The people inside wanted to get out and those outside wanted to get back in. Everyone was crying and yelling. There wasn't a policeman anywhere. Then two more bombs went off. You couldn't stay on the bus. But there was nowhere else. Oh god. *(Fights to control herself.)* Then somethin hit me. *(Checks upper arm.)* Here. See. This big red mark. *(Simon doesn't look.)* Those boys had started throwing stones. Rocks! I was so frightened. I ducked behind someone and then I crawled under the bus and out the other side. I just ran and ran and ran, as fast as I could, till I got to that little corrugated iron wall. I've never been so frightened in my life. That's when I saw you. *(She stares at him.)* Why did they do it? I mean it was the Red Cross! They were just fact-finding!

DEVOTEES IN THE GARDEN OF LOVE
by Suzan-Lori Parks
A garden in the middle of nowhere
Lily, a teeny tiny old woman in a wedding dress, 50-60

Lily and her daughter, George, watch from above as men do battle for George's hand in marriage. Lily is unimpressed with the protocol of modern warfare and here recalls a time in her youth that was far more idyllic.

LILY: My day we had messengers. Skinny mens and womens who earned uh cent or two by running up and down thuh hillside. Im my year I had me uh particular favorite. Nothin but bones by thuh time it was all through. That messenger came rippin up here at all hours. In thuh dead uh night! In thuh crack uh dawn! Would report -- you know -- thuh important stuff. Who said what, reinact ThissuhBody's troop's last gasp or show me how one uh ThatuhBody's troopers kept walkin for hours with uh flag run through their guts and how thuh run through flag had pinned uhnother tuh his back so he was walking for two -- with one piggy back, you know. Like uh shishkebob. That messengers speciality was thuh death throes. Kept us in stitches up here showing us who dropped dead and how. And they was droppin dead down there like flies drop so that messenger kept busy. Runned up here tuh tell me thuh news. Whuduhnt nothin but bones by battles end. Last time that message-er runned up here just his bones was doin thuh runnin and thuh stuff that holded thuh bones tughether was all used up as fuel tuh get them bones up thuh hill. We didnt bury thuh messenger. Gave him uh higher honor. My corset is from them messenger bones, you know. In my day we didnt waste.

24

DEVOTEES IN THE GARDEN OF LOVE
by Suzan-Lori Parks
A garden in the middle of nowhere
Madame Odelia Pandhar, a panderer, 40-60

A woman of many talents, Madame Odelia here reports from the "front," where divided camps of men do battle for the hand of her protegee.

MADAME ODELIA: Rat uh tat tat and kerblam berblooey. As someone said long ago: "The fighting words." That adage today has well proven true. There is only one way to describe the scene here the scene that began shortly over 5 days ago and seems well intended to last at least through the night. What began as what could be characterized as a border skirmish, a simple tribal dispute, has erupted into a battle of major consequence. High high up above me is the encampment of the bride-who'll-be who has been keeping watch on this situation. The actual area of our attention is not high high up but right down here right down here in, so to speak, "the thick of it". In the area just behind me through this thick veil of dead deadly smoke you can just make out the shapes of the 2 opposing camps and of course we are speaking of the camps of ThisOne and the camps of ThatOne. The two suitors vying for the hand of Miss George the beautiful most sought after bride-who'll-be who watches now from high above us with her mother, Ms. Mother Lily, from that far high hilltop. There is one word that, I guess you could say, sums up this brilliant display this passionate parade of severed arms and legs, genitals and fingertips, buttocks and heads, the splatterment the dismemberment, the quest for an embrace for the bride-who'll-be which has, for many, ended in an embrace of eternity, and that one word I think we could say that one word is "Devotion". This is Ms. Odelia Pandahr. At the Front.

25

THE END OF THE DAY
by Jon Robin Baitz
Malibu, the Present
Helen, 30's

Massey and Helen have just separated. Massey is an opportunist.
Helen wants some answers.

HELEN: Did you ever love me, Graydon?

[**MASSEY:** Ah. Well. Love. Well. Yes. Did I ever love you?
Did I? *(Beat.)* Yes, Helen, have no doubt in your mind. I did.]

HELEN: But sweetheart. You see, I don't think I can believe
you. I need to know. See. Here we are and -- I have been
trashed all my life. I respected you, Graydon, so please, don't
lie to me. Tell me the truth. Look at me and do that. Did you
ever love and respect me? Did you learn anything from me?
Did I give you succor and warmth? What were you thinking
when you hid in my chest at night, scared? Were we partners
together? *(Pause.)*

Did you seek out my company over all others? *(Beat.)*

Did you ever feel like excluding the outside world? Did
anything I say have any effect on your internal life? Did you
sometimes stop in the middle of the goddamn day, Graydon
and wonder what I was doing or feeling? Did you -- love me?
(Beat.)

Because I replay this thing in my head here and what I get to is
that this marriage was a sad and -- and -- and -- decorous little
affair -- and what offends me -- is that I do not believe you have
answered me. Understand what is lost. I have had the last ten
years of my life revealed to me as an absolute disaster, a con,
and a fraud. So can't you do me the humane fucking courtesy
of telling me in fact whether there was any love whatsoever? It
would make it so much better -- to know. *(Beat.)*

If you know how much I hate myself for having let you lie to
me for so long, I hate myself so much that it cancels out even
blaming you. Oh, Graydon. Because what I've come up with is

26

so interesting. And it never occurred to me consciously until this morning when I was eating my pasta. What I think is this: (*Pause*.)

I think you married me so as to become an American citizen.

[MASSEY: Yes. It's true, of course, my darling.]

HELEN: (*Smiles*.) And yet I loved you, is the rub. So silly. It's like loving a machine that swallows heat and energy but does nothing at all. And, and -- the only man I ever slept with. It's ... crazy. To have loved like this. I am...curious, we know I'm a dumb Jap blond, we know it but how do you sleep with someone for ten years? Wake up in the morning, the bad breath, the smells, the life, someone who -- basically -- offends you? (*Beat*.)

What -- what is it that could make you so dead inside that you could waste so much of yourself? I just don't understand that.

ESCAPE FROM HAPPINESS
by George F. Walker
The worn down kitchen of an old house
in the east end of a large city, the Present
Mary Ann, a woman trying to keep her family together

After her parents' home is invaded by a couple of thugs, Mary
Ann entertains one of the investigating police officers with her
theory on what she believes will save her dysfunctional family.

MARY ANN: Is this family doomed. I used to ask myself that
question all the time. Are we forever doomed. Forever on the
brink of destruction. Under some enormous shadow. Has God
constructed a gigantic, mean-spirited shadow full of noxious,
evil vibrations emanating poisonous, soul-killing rays, that has
one job and one job only. To hover over this family and keep
us doomed. And then one day I asked myself, why would God
single out this family. And I knew right away that God
wouldn't. God just made the shadow. And like everything elese
that God made, the shadow has a mind of its own. The shadow
picked this family to hover over. I figured all this out a while
ago, and it came as a great relief. You see, I didn't have to
wonder anymore how we'd displeased God. I could forget
about God for a while-which is always a great relief for me,
seeing how I feel basically that God hates me-Mustard?

[**DIAN:** No thanks.]

MARY ANN: Anyway, I could forget about God, and
concentrate on the shadow, and what possibly motivated it. You
see, the shadow is fate. And our fate, the fate of this family, has
some enormous grudge against us. So I figure we have to
appease it, make amends, make some kind of huge, almost
mythic, apology. We have to find a way of apologizing for
something we don't know we did. So it has to be symbolic. It
has to symbolize in some way everything bad each one of us
has ever done as an individual or as part of a group. It's an
almost impossible task. But we have to do it soon. Because
we're doomed. unless we make the shadow, you know, go away.
Events are unfolding here that prove we're running out of time.
Right now I'm making a chocolate cake, but inside what I'm
really doing is apologizing. This cake is an apology for all the

28

times I know that people I loved or people I hardly knew needed some special little treat, and I didn't have energy to make them one. Just a little thing. But you see this huge, symbolic apology will actually be made from thousands and thousands of little things just like this... This cake... This chocolate cake, and oatmeal cookies, and blueberry pancakes, fudge, a nicely pressed pair of slacks, a bit of change to someone in need, taking care of a friends's cat, smiling on the subway. These are the things that are going to save this family.

THE EVIL DOERS
by Chris Hannan
Glasgow, the Present
Tracky, a heavy metal fan, 15

Tracky's mother is an alcoholic and her father is a fast-talking cab driver. Here, she shares some of the darkness of their domestic life with an uncaring friend.

TRACKY: *(Tracky speaks to Susan's unlistening back.)* You should see him when he cries. That's the worst. I can't look. Because see human flesh, see when it's burned, see when it's grilled and the skin's like healing up and then it starts to cry, it starts to leak like these really disgusting tears? That's how *obsequious* he is. Same last night. I'm lying in my bed listening. I can hear him. Her. Then it goes quiet. *(Quiet.)*

Then it goes quiet. Tha's the worst. It goes quiet and my stomach turns to mud, because I know. Then the door opens and - shouting - and she's pushing the door in his face but then she runs down the corridor and *that's* when my stomach turns to mud - not when I said - *then* - and she's in the bathroom and locked the door. And he's after her, he's outside the door like begging her and saying he's sorry, and I just switch off. *(A taxi door slams, then another.)*

I just switch off. And then he's got his face up against the bathroom window - Agnes, Agnes - and she smashes right into it with a hammer. *(Taxi goes.)*

Then it's morning. You wake up clear as a bell and you think what happened?

FOUR PLAY
by *Gina Barnett*
Here and Now
Gert, a sweet and unassuming woman, 30's

When a new man in her life asks Gert to tell him about two of her favorite lovers from the past, she offers the following descriptions.

GERT: Amy Ingersoll, age eight. She lived next door. We played doctor together for two years by examining what we called our tinklers in a dark closet with a pen flashlight. When I was eight she came over to break the news that we couldn't play doctor together any more. Something deep inside her told her it was wrong and might cause her mother to get sick and die. I knew heartbreak for the first time. *(Sam yawns.)*

Joey Festiggi. Eleven. He was the first boy in our grade to have facial hair. A soft brown fuzz that hung over his top lip like a cloud. It made him look very dangerous. He smoked Camel straights. And he could burp on cue. He was an artist trapped in the body of a hood. *(She nods.)*

Nobody knew cause he was a hood and I was a nerd and it would've been bad for both of our images. But none of the hoody girls would go as far as me, and none of the nerdy guys knew that lips were for more than keeping your teeth warm in winter.

31

FREE RIDE ON THE QUEEN MARY
by Kate Moira Ryan
The deck of a ship
Anastasia, a woman with a questionable past, 30-40

Here, a woman claiming to be the missing Russian princess
describes, among other things, how she came to be in possession
of Rasputin's penis

ANASTASIA: I am the youngest daughter of Czar Nicholas
II. The one that escaped execution. I live with my common law
commoner of a husband in a trailer park on the Louisiana
border of Deadwood, Texas. In the beginning, life wasn't easy
there. I had never cooked nor cleaned before, but I got a
subscription to Good Housekeeping and T.V. Guide and I
adjusted. My name is Grand Duchess Anastasia Nicolaivna or if
you prefer Mrs. Wyatt J. Peppersnap, Jr. *(She takes out a
picture of an Elvis impersonator.)* I'm doing this job so Wyatt
can finally pay homage to the King at Graceland. So tips are
appreciated. Now the lacing of the roller blades is like a
scientific procedure. *(She puts on rubber gloves.)* I learned
how to rollerblade on the deck of my father's Yacht, The
Standart. My father was assassinated by the Bolsheviks as was
my entire immediate family at Ekaterinburg. I managed to
escape not through my own wits. I had fallen in dead faint and
my sister, Grand Duchess Tatiana shielded me from the bullets
with her body. When I woke up and the smoke had cleared...I
was not killed. A young solider who was quite bessotten with
me, and Alexander Tschiakovsky smuggled me out to
Bucharest, raped me and married me upon the arrival of his
child with whom I wanted no association. My husband, this
soldier, was murdered in the streets some say for protecting me
others say for selling Anastasia icons on the black market made
from strands of my hair, finernail clippings and various incisors.
However, widowhood was not for this Grand Duchess. I made
my way to the land of opportunity and was lucky in love the
second time around. When I first met my second husband,
Wyatt at the Dew Drop Inn, he was intimidated by the manners I
had acquired at the Russian Court. He had never met a woman
who drank vodka straight from the bottle with a straw. And I
had never met a man as virile as he, except for Rasputin, but
that's a whole other can of worms or maybe jar. *(Takes out a*

jar with a Jeff Stryker penis in it.) Rasputin's. Yup! Still works. Any takers? It is one of my most cherished possessions as you can imagine, but I gotta get Wyatt to Graceland before the cancer gets him. Who wants to help me grant Wyatt's last wish? *(Opens jacket.)* I also, have some autographed pictures, *(Takes out a similar jar.)* and I'll throw in the eye ball of my father. Still as sea blue as it was. I'll give it all to you for fifty bucks. Yes, Fifty Bucks any takers?

GERTRUDE, QUEEN OF DENMARK
by *Pat Kaufman*
Elsinore Castle
Ophelia, a madwoman, 18-20
In this comic retelling of <u>Hamlet</u>, Ophelia is rescued from the
pond and here recounts her experiences to Queen Gertrude.

OPHELIA: One of those awful players was on the banks of the
river counting his gold coins that Hamlet gave him for
butchering the true script. Like he butchered my father. Oh,
Hamlet! That player saw me fall in the pond, my white gown all
innocent dragging me down, his breath all foul from whiskey
and rotting teeth he called me Hold! Hold on! Those players
never have time to take good care of themselves they're always
on the road, a noxious bunch of fellows, ill bred and low class.
But, being some sort of artist, maybe with a flicker of light in his
soul, he pulled me out of the wet and tried to sooth me with a
tale of romance.....An amazing and chilling tale he played in
London about an Italian family so insane for revenge.....They
tried to part the lovers and the girl drank a potion and.....

[**GERTRUDE:** She is marvelously like her father in endless
speech.]

OPHELIA: A poison potion. And she drank the whole thing.
And she seemed dead as a stone....."Through all her veins did
run a cold and drowsie humor.....No warmth no breath did
testify she livest, the roses in her lips and cheeks did fade....."
But actually she was living.

[**JANE:** Oh cruel!]

[**GERTRUDE:** Oh scary!]

OPHELIA: The audiences went fainting from their stalls in
terror. However, the player said, the amazing part was that such
a fantasticological brew could be found in real life and he
would get some for me. If I wanted him to. Did I want him to?
It made my pulse race as a ship being carried forward in a high
wind onto the shoals. I was almost too scared to say yes. But
then I thought, it's now or never, my heart is broken anyway, my
reason scattered, it's hardly worth living--I'll give it a try!

34

GULF WAR
by Joyce Carol Oates
A suburban home, the Present
Nicole, a woman struggles to cope with reality, 20's-30's

Following the death of her baby, Nicole sinks into alcoholism and numb despair. Here, she describes her apathy to the audience.

NICOLE: I've been married for six and half years, and I've been in love at least that long. *(Pause.)* Or longer! *(Pause.)* You don't chose your fate. I used to think you did--we did--but we <u>don't</u>. Fate chooses <u>us</u>. *(Pause.)* I used to be the 'weather girl' for South Orange, new Jersey cable T.V. channel 39--but that was a long time ago. I drew mixed notices from the viewers: O.K. with the good, sunny weather, 'smiles too much' with the bad. They see through you if you smile wrong, but they sure don't like you if you don't smile. *(Pause.)* Stuart's right: whatever it is, it 'enters through the eyes.' (*Pause as if bitterly.)* That's our fate.

There's the 'Gulf War' going on right now--in the T.V. downstairs in the family room. This is the time of the 'Gulf War'--but I'm not political. *(Pause.)*

You can be not political like you can be...not a mother, for instance. *(Pause.)*

I am not political and have no interest in the Gulf War or in any war. I lack the spirit of...optimism. *(Pause.)* A depletion of optimism. *(Pause.)* 'Depletion of oxygen'--did I say? *(More firmly.)* 'Depletion of optimism.' *(Pause.)*

I was eleven years old when the Vietman War officially ended without my knowing it and I was through with my schooling including three semesters at Connecticut College by the time 'an awakened interest in the Vietman War became a trendy phenomenon in American education and entertainment'--that goes for the Holocaust, too. *(Pause.)* I do not care for war movies, of any era.

INFIDELITIES

by Richard Zajdlic

A home in England, the Present

Jenny, a woman frustrated by life as a military wife, 20-30

Jenny has been unable to communicate honestly with her husband since his stationing in Northern Ireland. Here, she speaks the truth into a tape recorder.

JENNY: *(Jenny's house: she is recording a cassette to Brian.)* Monday 18th. 11:30 a.m. Hello. Me again. How's things? I'm...I'm... *(She switches off.)* I'm bored! Bored, bored, bored, bored, bored! *(She switches on.)* I'm fine. Everything's fine back here. Still helping out at the Nursery. We're taking them all to the Zoo next week. A day out at last - my God! *(She switches off.)* My God. All those bored animals in cages. Watching them. Watching me. Lucky them. Who'd pay to see my life? *(She switches on.)* So that'll be good. *(Pause.)* I'm having sex with the T.V. repair man at the moment. *(She laughs, switching it off.)* No. Can't say that. Can't say anything really. *(She switches on.)* Dear Bri. I have nothing whatsoever to say to you. Love Jenny. *(She switches off. She lights a cigarette, remembers the baby and stubs it out irritatedly. She switches the recorder on.)* Jenny's tape. 11:40 a.m. Dear Bri. how are the Irish tarts? Keeping you warm nights? Oh no, I forgot. You're not going to do that anymore, are you? Me neither. No more T.V. repair men for me. Got myself quite nicely out of that one, didn't I? Made you feel a right bastard while I came out smelling of roses. Good for me. Good old Jenny Collins - liar and adulteress extraordinaire. You see Bri, you were right. I have been having an affair. It doesn't matter who, tho' it's certainly not the T.V. repair man. Oh, don't worry, it's over now. It didn't last long...it wasn't what I expected either. It made me feel even lonelier - isn't that peculiar? I still feel detached, distant from everyone, though the two weeks we had toghether helped. Thawed me out, I suppose. Tho' it was better when we didn't talk. I felt closer then. The silence was...comforting. Talking was bad. All brick walls and boxes. The silence isn't comforting anymore. I get scared now. I want you to talk to me now. Phone, letters, tape, anything. I hold your jumpers at night, did you know that? *(She is crying. She switches off.)* Don't stop. Don't for Christ's sake, stop. *(She* *switches on.)* I. Am. So. Unhappy. Bri. I am so unhappy with you. With me. My life. D'you ever wonder what happens when you go away? Nothing. Life just stops for me. All I do is go through the motions, waiting for you to come back so I can start again. I want more than that. There's more than that for me. Wasting my life. The sheer bloody waste!

When I look at myself, what I've become, I get so angry. And yes, I do blame you Bri. Unreasonable, I know, but I think I'd be a very different person if I hadn't met you. Not better. Not necessarily better. But different. And I resent that.

Even now, what I'm saying, what I'm trying to say. Selfish cow, I'm thinking - me, me, me, me! Wrapped up in my own self-pitying little world. Get out, then. Do it. Be different. I've tried that haven't I? I've tried him. I don't want him. I want you. I want more of you.

D'you know, sometimes I say things to you, really nasty things. Things I know will hurt just to get a reaction. Just to get inside you and start us talking, fighting, loving again. We drift on so easily, you and me. Not noticing things. Things like we aren't working anymore. All the talk, endless drivel, it's just echoes. Echoes from a long time ago. From when it all meant something.

There's part of you I can't reach anymore. That you've shut off, held back, 'this part's mine so hands off'. Can't you see that's why we fail? Why you're so lonely, why I'm so empty. You've built a barrier between us and all that makes me do is draw up one of my own and believe me Bri, that hurts.

We're married. We're partners, not opponents. We've got a child - son, daughter, whatever it is I spew out my belly it's ours. And it's relying on us to work this out. You've got to choose, Bri. Sooner or later you have to decide. You can't run off to your precious Army for ever and we'll still be here long after they've chewed you up and spat you out. Your future is me. Believe that, Bri. We belong. Don't you feel that? To each other. And we have to change if we want it to work. Don't shake your head. Don't tell me you can't change, that it's just the way you are and always will be, that's crap! You're not the man I married. And I'm a million miles away from the girl you fell in love with.

37

We're different people now and we've got to make allowances for that. Compromise. This mindless trench warfare that says I'm damned if I'm giving any more of me away first. It's stupid! We can't give up. We can't just walk away. Where to? We owe our baby more than that. I love you, Bri. *(Laughs.)* D'you know, once upon a time that used to mean, I love you, Bri. Now all it really means is help. *(She switches off. Presses rewind. Pause.)* Help me. *(The tape stops. She presses record again.)* Monday 18th. 12 o'clock. Hello. Me again. How's things? I'm fine. Everything's fine back here. Just fine.

JAR THE FLOOR
by Cheryl L. West
Lakeland, Illinois, the Present
Madear, 90

At her 90th birthday party Madear hallucinates that her husband, Man, who left her when she was young, is returning.

MADEAR: *(Overlapping, can be heard before she's seen.)* Man? Man, is dat you callin' for me? Man? I'm comin'. *(Entering. She has draped Lola's boa on her shoulder and is wearing Lola's hat and carrying Lola's purse. She has smeared lipstick across her face, and is tapping her cane on the floor as if she's looking for something.)* See, I'm ready...Man you ain't dead. You didn't leave me. *(Crying.)* You didn't leave me here all by myself...Jar de floor...See, I'm pretty now...like Lola Bit. You gon' dance wid me Man? *(Attempts a step or two.)* See, I can dance now...I ain't ugly no more. I'm pretty like Lola...Come on now Man, jar de floor...Please...I know you didn't leave me...jar de floor... *(Lola stops talking, Vennie begins to stomp her foot, softly at first and then louder. MayDee eventually joins in. Lola hangs up the phone, joins in and then Raisa.)* I know you's wid me, Man. You didn't leave me here all by myself...(The stomping continues, she turns around and looks at them as if she's seeing them for the first time.)* I cain't half hear ya'll chil'ren. Let me feel you. *(The stomping builds as the heartbeat between the generations resounds loudly.)* Ya'll chil'ren better jar de floor. Yes Lord, jar dat floor.

39

LA MAISON SUSPENDUE

by Michel Tremblay

A log cabin house at Duhamel, Quebec, the Present, 1950
Albertine, a woman locked in conflict with her brother, 41

A family holiday in the country gives disapproving Albertine an
opportunity to confront her brother about his homosexuality.

ALBERTINE: *(Same tone as her mother.)* You don't know
what you do to me, Édouard, hein, you really don't know! You
don't realize how everything you represent makes me sick! You
play with me, you play with my reactions to your stupid
nonsense, but you don't realize how serious it is, how really
serious it is! When you come through the door, on Saturday
night, for your weekly visit, and I hear your goddammed voice,
which is never the same, I tell myself I've no idea who you're
gonna look like this time, and all I want to do is run out the
back door and down the alley! Have you ever stopped to think,
Édouard, that none of us in the house knows who you are? We
don't know! The other women on la rue Fabre, when they see
their brothers come up the street from la rue Mont-Royal, they
say: tiens, v'lá mon frére Émile, or v'lá mon Frére Albert...Not
me! One Saturday night it's Juliette Pétrie who comes
sauntering up the street, and the next Saturday, it's Shirley
Temple with a dress that's too short or La Poune with her little
cap...Sometimes it's the neighbours, Édouard, who tell me: tiens,
v'lá votre frére, and I want to spit in their faces because I'm
afraid of whatever it is that's coming! In the winter it's not so
bad...I don't get my surprise til you're in the kitchen and I can
hide my shame in the oven, pretending to baste the roast of
pork, but in the summer, Édouard, in the summer, it's the whole
of la rue Fabre that sees you coming...I see you come up the
street the same time as everyone else and there's no way I can
hide my shame! The whole world can see the shame on my
face! *(She screams.)* If you don't take off those ridiculous
pyjamas and put on something decent, I'm going to rip them off
your back and you'll have to go fish them up from the end of
the dock! *(She is trembling.)*

THE LAST ACT IS A SOLO
by Robert Anderson
The shabby, cluttered one-room apartment
of an elderly actress, the Present
Laura Cunningham, once, one of the "great ladies of
the American Theatre", 80's

Laura is forced to face the reality that she can no longer care for
herself. Her nephew has found a home for her near his own, and
she here reveals to him her fears and feelings about the future.

LAURA: If you want to see me, come in here. I'm not going
out there. *(Addressing the chair.)* My dog, Console. *(Spells.)*
C-O-N-S-O-L-E.. And she is my consolation. Ten years ago
she was in a play with me. We became inseparable. Neither of
us has worked since...She's my dearest friend. I'm staying alive
for her. It's my gift to her, a not inconsiderable gift,
considering...When I die, they'll just put her away. Like the
Egyptians. *(Calls off.)* Yes, they will. So you mind you P's and
Q's. She's deaf. She doesn't hear half of what I say. But then I
don't hear half of what she says. She mumbles...Yes, you do.
*(Turning her attention back to the "interviewer," She suddenly
puts her hands over her face.)* Oh, no pictures, please!

I told them, "No pictures"... Five years ago I lost my
cheekbones. *(Her hands come down.)* If you want a picture,
take one of these. *(She touches the stack of photographs on the
table.)* Can you believe it? People still send me pictures to be
autographed...I don't know where they get them. *(She looks at
one or two, wistfully.)* You might take one and give it to your
obituary people. Your paper has always run such terrible
pictures of me...I think it's because fifty years ago I wrote a
naughty note to your critic...*(After a last fond glance at
pictures, she puts them down...All business.)* I assume you're
here because you've heard I might be doing a movie. I'm
expecting the director...*(Vague wave towards the door. A little
taunting.)* I'm surprised your paper is interested in me at all. A
month ago they ran an article on the Distinguished Veteran
Actresses, Stars for whom there were no parts in modern
plays...and they didn't mention me. *(She feels she has
scored...smiles.)* Ah, well...
    "No memory of having starred

Atones for later disregard,
Or keeps the end from being hard."

Robert Frost. I was sent to college by a dear rich woman from Boston who said that if I didn't marry her son, she would send me to college...I had no intention of marrying her son. He was just very taken with my breasts. I matured early. Boys were always trying to do something to come in contact with my breasts. Brushing up against me accidentally, pushing, wrestling. Strangely, I never had any sensation there. I used to say to men, "If it please you..." Coming from the wrong side of town, i couldn't afford an education. So I accepted. *(Pauses.)* After the second year in college, I went as an apprentice to a summer theatre, sweeping the stage, painting scenery. I also played a small but very good part in a new play that was trying out. That fall I went to New York with the play...and the playwright. *(SHE smiles archly.)* And the rest is...*(A gesture.)* The last offer of work I had was to do a commercial for dentures. The deal fell throught when they found I had my own teeth. Impossible as it is to believe, it seems there's something called "Truth in Advertising." *(She chuckles.)* Ten years ago after that standing ovation at The Tony Awards, people scurried around trying to come up with a play for me. Nothing but sentimental trash. It seems that by the time a writer is old enough to know what old age is about, he's too old to write a play. *(She muses a moment.)* For a while I was in great demand for those "standing ovation" appearances. If they felt the season had been dull and they were in for a dreary awards show...*(Gesture.)* "Ladies and gentlemen, Miss Laura Cunningham." *(Without rising she stretches out her arms and bows low...and then with her arms indicates an audience rising.)* I became Miss Laura Cunningham when I turned seventy. I think it's the American equivalent of the British Dame..."Rise, Miss Laura Cunningham"...It was nice for a while...The Oscars..*(She repeats the bow, and the audience rising.)* The Emmys...*(The same.)* The New York Film Festival. *(The same.)* You know when I was acting, I never received a standing ovation. *(She beams at the irony.)* And then when I was getting the ovations, I couldn't get a job. *(A gesture, a shake of the head..."no sense to it.")* I did rather enjoy one summer when I was the entertainment of The Queen Elizabeth. One round trip. Free passage, and all I had to do was one night each way give a little talk before the movies began. Good evening, Ladies and Gentlemen. I am

Laura Cunningham. I've been asked to talk to you about my life in the theatre...I wasn't asked back. I think the Captain wanted some pretty jiggly young thing to sit at his table and tell the passengers about her days as a starlet...both of them. *(Turns towards the kitchen.)* Console?...Console?... There have been some nights I was sure might be her last. The other night I put a small crucifix in her bed when I said good-night... The next morning I found it by my bedroom slippers, as though she were saying, "You die!"... We're both more than ready to "excuse ourselves." *(A gesture, raising her arm as if in "farewell." With a sly smile, she takes from her pocket a small silver pill box and holds it up and rattles the pills inside.)* Some years ago, a very dear friend of mine was dying. His doctor gave him three pills. "Kenneth, if you're in pain, take one pill. If the pain is severe, take two. I wouldn't advise you take three" ...He didn't take any...They talk about the serenity of old age. Nonsense! I didn't know any serenity in my old age till Kenneth gave me these the day before he died. They gave Kenneth the courage to die, and me the courage to live. Without them...*(Shakes her head.)* Now if the day should come when I think I'm losing my marbles...Or...whatever...*(A gesture, finger to lips.)* All off the record...

THE LAST ACT IS SOLO
by Robert Anderson
The shabby, cluttered one-room apartment
of an elderly actress, the Present
Laura Cunningham, once, one of the "great ladies of
the American Theatre, 80's

Laura is forced to face the reality that she can no longer care for
herself. Her nephew has found a home for her near his own, and
she here reveals to him her fears and feelings about the future.

LAURA: I don't want anyone to take care of me. Nobody has
ever had to take care of me! *(After a moment, she turns and
looks at Ben.)* I'm sorry. You've been so good to me. I don't
know why. I never did anything for you.

[**BEN:** That's not true.]

LAURA: *(A wan smile.)* Will you invent something new to
eat? *(She starts to cry again.)*

[**BEN:** We'll find something...There'll be something.]

LAURA: *(Straightening up...calming.)* Old women take care
of children. I had no children. I'm no good with children.
Even on stage I was no good with children. *(A small smile.)* A
few years ago, I offered my services to a Drama School...for
nothing. I thought it might be nice for young actresses to come
here for an afternoon. I could serve them tea and talk to them
about art and life...They said, "Thank you, but no." They said
they'd be glad to have me come to graduation so that they could
honor me. *(An outburst.)* I don't want to be honored. I want to
work!

[**BEN:** Laura, you've worked all your life. Look at this room.
(He gestures to the posters and pictures...her "life.")]

LAURA: *(She has been thinking...an idea.)* Maybe there's a
new captain on the Queen Elizabeth...There are women, you
know, old women like me, who cruise forever. ...Their trunks
are hauled off one ship and taken across the pier to another.
They sail back and forth, back and forth forever...I could do

44

that. I would pay my way by doing what I've always done, entertaining people. People love theatre..."Good evening ladies and gentlemen..." *(Unconsciously, She straightens a bit and puts on her "manner".)* "I was Laura Cunningham...I've been asked to talk to you for a few minutes before the movie begins, about my life in the theatre..." *(She stops...The facade breads, and she bows her head.)*

LIPS TOGETHER TEETH APART
by Terrence McNally
A beach house on Fire Island, the Present
Chloe, a woman trying to salvage a ruined weekend, 30-40

Chloe's husband, John, has been sleeping with her brother's wife. When both couples spend the 4th of July together, the close proximity of her rival causes Chloe to suffer a momentary lapse of her usual cheerfulness.

CHLOE: He's right, Sam. But before I go into my six-hour exile *(Joyfully! I'll get the second act down pat)*, I think you should know something about me. All of you. I think it is precisely the small things I run on about and that seem to annoy you so - the little day-to-day details, the nuances - that give our lives some zip and some meaning. I care about cooking the burgers so each of you get exactly what you ask for. I worry about who's driving the children's car pool that particular week. I notice what's going on around me, every detail. I don't miss a thing. I've got all your numbers. I talk too much, probably because it's too horrible to think about what's really going on. You should try it, Miss Broody-Woody, Miss Highfalutin! You think you're so superior. Well maybe you are. But to whom? Me? Honey, just about anyone is superior to me. You're going to have to do a lot better than that if you want to keep that attitude up. I'll try to think of something lofty to say at dinner. *(She starts to go to her room, then turns back.)* You know, I'm not mad at any of you. Really. I think we're all pathetic. Sally, will you clean up? We'll have bugs galore. Pussy Galore! Remember her?

(She goes into her room and lies down on her bed.)

MAN, WOMAN, DINOSAUR
by Regina M. Porter
Present
50's, a maid

Bernadette responds to her son Li'l Samuel who tells her that his daddy is better than she is.

BERNADETTE: I was eighteen. The youngest of four girls. All my Mama seemed to spit out was girls; girls who married; girls who worked; girls who died young. And there goes me. The country, my place to be. Food to cook. Clothes to wash. Enough chores to make anyone grow old young. That didn't fit into my permanent plan. I had bigger things in mind. Away type things. Then comes grave-digging, Mr. Marsh. Setting his mind on me. Setting his life on me. I called him fool. I laughed him fool. Said out and out I wanted better. Even when folks about town got to telling me that I oughtn't to put him off that way, I shrugged them off and kept straight ahead, working, saving, to get away and do better. He came one night. Like a zoro, rooty bad. And dragged me out of my own house. On a tombstone--naked--for three nights I laid. Tied and gagged--I laid. You ever seen a graveyard at night? Or the spirits there? You did, you'd know shouldn't nobody be dead. It's sad and lonely dead. All they talk about is loneliness. And lost love; the dead. (*Pause.*) I'd see old women, antebellum white. They's slither their way out of the black dirt, holding on to the shreds of their crinoline skirts like it was still a fine thing and not the patches of nothing it really was. They's come to me with their dainty, skeleton smiles and say, "Young Lady, you've got to love that man." I'd see relatives of mine, cousins from slavery times, their hands and feet bound with shackles that rang like bells every time they moved. They didn't like my situation much. But in chains and shackles, what could they do--except tell me to love that man? The worst were the children. Infants. Babies. Cut short from life. They'd crawl around the graveyard on their hands and knees. A few would find their way to me. Sidle on top of me, wanting milk not in my breast to give. And when they realized I

47

was all empty, they'd cry like you wouldn't believe. But it made perfect sense to me. *Love*...They too were telling me I had to love that man. (*Pause.*) On the third day, your Daddy came. He fucked me. He washed me. He fed me figs and cheese. And I loved that man. But just 'cause I loved the father, who says I've got to love the son?

MARINER
by Don Nigro
The flagship of Christopher Columbus, 1942
Juana, the mad daughter of Ferdinand and Isabella, 20's-30's

When King Ferdinand declares Columbus to be insane, the famous
sailor asks Juana if she share's her father's opinion. The mad
princess offers the following reply.

JUANA: I'm not sure I'm the best person to ask, Christopher.
The study of Latin and sexual intercourse have left me insane,
amo, amas, amat, and I'm gratful to you and Julius Caesar for
this. My mother had ten children, and they all died but me, and
I was the one she liked the least. I married Philip the
Handsome, and gave birth to Emperors, but he loved other
women, and when Mother died I became the Queen of Hearts,
but Father rules for me, while I stay in the palace, running
around naked and visiting the grave of my husband, who has
become a very properous worm farm. I have sex with my dead
husband's ghost in the cemetery. He's a much better lover now
that he's dead, but I think he betrays me with the other corpses.
What was the question again?

[**COLUMBUS:** Do you think I'm insane?]

JUANA: This is something I've thought seriously about. The
thing is, there's different kinds of madness. There's the more
common, destructive madness, that distorted and unorthodox
way of looking at the world which results in tyranny and
violence, physical and psychological, to others and to one's self.
Then there's the much more rare, creative madness, that
distorted and unorthodox way of looking at the world which
results in creation, exploration and discovery. The problem is
that to ordinary, normal people, they look like pretty much the
same thing, which is why some of the best books and people in
the world tend to get thrown on bonfires. Myself, I travel
through my insanity as on a wondrous voyage. Perhaps you
should be that kind of explorer, Christopher - instead of sailing
back and forth across the ocean, go inside your ears. It's much
more satisfying in your head, the possibilities are infinite, and
you don't have to worry so much about barnacles.

THE MONKEY BUSINESS
by David Bottrell
A luncheon meeting of the Friends of
the Primate House Women's Committee, the Present
Adele Gaither, a dedicated chairwoman, 30-50

At the close of her term as chairwoman of the Friends of the Primate House Women's Committee, Adele addresses the general membership and lists the accomplishments of her administration.

ADELE: Well, Connie, it has indeed been a wonderful two years. Why the memories just flood my head when I think about all that we have accomplished in these last two years. To finally see these wonderful creatures freed from the bondage of cages and bars and instead placed in spacious, beautiful invironmental enclosures, fllled with natural looking trees and rocks. Where the animal kingdom and human beings can come into close contact with each other without actually touching. Separated only by large panes of reinforced glass.

Why I remember when my husband, Arthur, and I walked through the hallways for the very first time, I could not help but weep. At the sight of the orangutangs happily swinging from tree to tree. At the colorful murals painted on the walls of the enclosures depicting the beautiful African looking landscapes. And I felt proud. Proud that the Friends of the Primate House Women's Committee was able to band together, overcome our differences, and bring this beautiful building into exlstance.

Oh, it wasn't all a bed of roses. Right girls? No, there were many thorns and briars along the way. The seemlingly endless delays in constructlon, the red tape, the eternal struggle to raise the money. Why I remember when I was working day and night to stuff invitations to our Gorilla Fund picnic, my own mother said to me, "Adele, What do you care about a bunch of monkeys?" She did, she said that to me. And I looked her in the eye and said "Mother, It's not just about monkeys. It's about the earth and saving the many creatures, great and small, that God gave us. It's about saving them for our children, and our children's chlldren. And she sald to me, "But Adele, you don't have any children." And I said, "Mother, you didn't have to bring that up. But if you'll remember, Arthur has three children by his first marriage, and I want to leave them a world where they'll be able to see a red tailed Orangutang whenever they want to. And then she said if Arthur's children ever wanted to see red tailed orangutangs all they had to do was look in the mirror. Can you imagine? My own mother.

But I didn't let that stop me. We went on with our Gorilla Fund Picnic and it was, as you all remember, a great success. As was our Adopt A Chimpanzee Campaign, and let's not forget the triumph of the Baboonathon. Our breeding program has been a dynamic force in bringing together these rare creatures and saving them from extinction. The culmination of this wonderful program came last week wlth the birth of a healthy female baboon rlght here in our own zoo. I am indeed pleased to be closing my tenure as chairwoman on thls happy, happy note. But there are many obstacles yet to be overcome. As many of you know, the city's fiscal problems threaten to close our beautiful primate house. Look around you and ask yourself: Where will these apes go? What will happen to them if this beautiful facility is closed. We will have to lobby long and hard if we are to save this wonderful institution. And the task of leading us in this battle is now falling upon the shoulders of our new chairwoman. And believe you me, I cannot think of a better person in whom to entrust this sacred mission.

Why, I remember when it looked like we wouldn't be able to afford that pair of black mountain gorillas, it was Charlotte, using her wonderful negotiating skills that she brings with her from the real estate field, not only got us both Gorillas at a reduced price, but even got them to throw in two spider monkeys and the price of shipping. She has been a tireless fighter and friend. I give you your new chairwoman, a crusader, a fighter, and a friend to primates everywhere. Charlotte Simpson Stinson.

MOTHER'S DAY
by Kate Aspengren
Here and Now
Esther, a woman who gave up her child

A woman recalls her teenage pregnancy.

ESTHER: I was sixteen years old. For awhile, I wondered what it might be like to keep her. After all, she was mine. But my parents said that if I kept her, I'd be ruining my life. And theirs, too, altought they never really said so. I knew that I had disappointed them.

My mother took my pregnancy very personally. She said it made her look like a terrible mother. A failure. Practically every time I looked up it seemed like she was staring at me, her eyes all wild and angry, like she just wanted a way to get me out of her house. My dad didn't get mad. But once he found out, he quit touching me. No more hugs. Just these occasional polite little pats on the shoulder. It felt like some stranger trying to get my attention so that he could ask for directions.

I was an average kid, I guess. Although in a school the size of mine, no one was really average. There were so few of us that we each had our own thing to be good at. Mine was band. I started playing the flute in the third grade and, by the time I was in junior high, I was better than all the high school flute players. Of course, there were only about five of them. But I was still better and they all hated me. I met my boyfriend, Ted, in band. He played trombone, but not very well. On my fifteenth birthday, he gave me a little silver flute on a necklace. I tought it was the most beautiful thing I'd ever seen. Ted was only the second boy I'd ever dated.

Bobby O'Halloran was the first. We actually only went out once, to a hay rack ride with the church youth group. He held my hand.

Accidentally.

He dropped his Baby Ruth bar in the hay and was feeling around for it when he grabbed my hand by mistake. I clutched

52

onto it for dear life and we stayed in this sort of sweaty death grip for the rest of the ride. Very romantic.

So, if you count Bobby, Ted was the second man in my life. Initially, we felt very grown-up to have created a child through all of our adolescent pawing and panting.

We talked about getting married; Ted was going to get a job at his father's paint store, I would finish high school, go to nursing school at St. Perpetua's over in Coldwater. We'd be the perfect young family, the pride of Watson's Chapel. The fantasies lasted about two days. Then we got frightened and angry and we broke up. We never spoke again, even when he was to sign the papers. After graduation, Ted married Betty Harrison, my next door neighbor. The had seven children. *(Esther laughs.)* I guess Ted never did figure out how birth control works.

MOTHER'S DAY

by Kate Aspengren

Here and Now

Mary, an adoptive mother, 60's

A woman remembers the day that she and her husband adopted an infant.

MARY: It was a Tuesday. Tuesday, May first. Mrs. Ryan called at about nine in the morning. "We have a baby for you, Mary. A little girl." A baby? *(She laughs.)* We got to the agency and they took us to a little room that had an old plaid couch and a painting of ducks and geese on the wall. It seemed like we waited there forever. I counted all the ducks in the painting, then all the geese, and was just starting in on the cattails when Mrs. Ryan came in carrying the littlest bundle of child I had ever seen. She handed her to me and said, "Here's your daughter." Then she left us alone. Our first time as a family. We didn't know what to do exactly; we were almost afraid to touch her. We uncovered her arms and she grabbed onto one of Andrew's fingers. He immediately turned to mush and stayed that way with her his entire life.

The pictures we have from that day are funny. We took turns taking each other's picture with the baby. It's hard to tell which of us looks more awkward with her. Andrew is holding her way out in front of him, like he's afraid he'll crush her if she gets too close. And I have my arm cocked with my elbow way up in the air as if I think she has to stay perpendicular. *(She demonstrates with the bear.)* We really didn't know what we were doing. My great aunt, Frieda, had warned us to be careful when we gave victoria her bath. "She's got no muscle control, you know. Hang onto her head so it doesn't bounce around or she'll get brain damage." We were terrified. That night, for her first bath, Andrew got out the baby book, turned to the chapter on bathing and read each step out loud to me while I followed his instructions. He held the book in his right hand and with his left he held Victoria's head like a ripe honeydew. *(Laughs.)* I have had a good life; some wonderful things have happened to me. But nothing has ever compared with the elation and the joy and the love that I felt when on the day we brought our daughter home.

54

MOVING
by *Lee Kalcheim*
A small apartment in New York, 1970 and 1976
Megan, a fallen Catholic looking for meaning in life, 23

Megan is an earthy young woman helping her friend to move into
a new apartment. Here, Megan tells Diana about her search for
God.

MEGAN: Can you imagine a combination more deadly than a
Jewish mother and an Irish Catholic father? One giveth and the
other taketh away.

[**DIANA:** I can't imagine you in a church.]

MEGAN: It wasn't easy. You know what my biggest problem
was? I thought I was smarter than all the priests. I had to hear
those dumb, dumb sermons. Y'know where the theme would be
something like, "Be good to your mother." I used to wise ass in
Sunday School. Finally, one of the priests called me in and
said, "Shea? What's your problem?" I said, "My problem is that
I don't believe any of this bullshit." I didn't say bullshit to the
priest...I said something like, "stuff. I don't believe any of this
stuff." He said, "What is it you don't believe?" I said, "Take
your pick." So he started, "Do you believe in the Father?"
"No." "The son?" "No." "The Holy Ghost?" "No." "Do you
belive in anything?" Tha's when I said, "Yes...confession!"
"How can you believe in confession?" I said, "'Cause it's a great
idea. It pre-dates Freud by twelve centuries." *(They both
laugh.)* So, I left the Church. Quit Catholic School. Mom
figured I was making the leap to Judaism. I told her, "Mom, I
don't believe in God in Three Places and I don't believe in God
in One Place. Religion's a crutch. I'm not gonna substitue one
crutch for another." Then, my mother says, dig this...she says,
"Megan, my child. Everybody's gotta have a crutch.
Everybody has to have a God. you don't want a Jewish God.
You don't want a Catholic God. You'll have a God someday.
Believe me." Well...if she's not right, she certainly kept me on
my toes, because there isn't a day that goes by that I don't wake
up and wonder if I'm going to find a God today. Maybe I do
have one. Maybe it's success. Or stability. I think I worship the
God of Stability. Pick a God. Any God.

MOVING
by Lee Kalcheim
A small apartment in New York, 1970 and 1976
Diana, a young woman seeking to
escape her affluent background, 21

Here, Diana tells her friend a story of an experience in her prep
school that changed her life.

DIANA: I'm sorry. This job thing is new to me. It's not just
my sex. Or my generation. Or my family. I mean...I went to a
Quaker school. Absolutely uncompetitive! We used to have an
Awards Ceremony at the end of the year. Everybody got an
award! Then it dawned on me, that if everybody got an award, it
didn't mean anything...So I went to the Headmaster and I told
him, "Why don't you give up the awards, altogether. I mean if
everybody gets an award, it doesn't mean anything." He looked
at me and said, "Diana, not everyone realized that. There are
boys and girls here who have never gotten an award in their life.
It means something to them. So for that reason, we do it." And
I said, "But don't you realize how condescending that is to
them. It's ultimately going to make them feel worse." He just
glared at me and said, "Miss Schmidt. Someday, somebody's
going to prick your bubble." I just...I couldn't help it. I burst
out laughing. So he called my mother.

[**MEGAN:** What did your mother say? I can't wait.]

DIANA: No. It's the one time I can remember that my mother
surprised me. She came into school. Came in looking like a
million dollars. Camel's hair coat. Blonde hair. Looked like a
Smith College undergrad. Came in smelling like an ocean
breeze. I looked at her and said to myself, "I'm gonna get it."
Mr. Dumwalt, the Headmaster, told her what I said...and Mom
took me aside. She sat me down...and said, "Don't worry about
Mr. Dumwalt. He was born with a pole up his ass!" I couln't
believe it. We laughed and laughed. Couldn't believe it. I think
that's one of the reasons, I've never abandoned hope for Mom.

NEVERTHELESS (Transition)
by Kenneth Bernard
A theatre, the Present
Woman, a performer, any age

Here, a woman responds to a list of unrelated words offered by the theatre manager by incorporating them into a disjointed speech.

WOMAN: *(A long ascending, controlled scream by the Woman, stopped suddenly, after which she recites, breathlessly.)* If I ever lived in Schenectady I'm sure I've forgotten it. The only thing Schenectadians ever do is eat naval oranges promptly at 4:52 every weekday. Or is that the bus Dad came home on after work? Mal á la téte! Mal á la téte! I screamed as he walked in. Walked in? It was a veritable rhythm, I can tell you. He came in like a conga, grabbing Mom's tits with an asinine grin and saying, "Are the parsnips sweetening?" Now what the hell was that all about? Two pieces of ectoplasm gearing up before supper even. My mother was an absolute stool when it came to him. Sat all over her. Mal á la téte! Mal á la téte! I would scream. She only drooled and said, "Libidinous old fool. You wouldn't know a parsnip if you ate one." And laughed like an udder idiot. That usually made him realize he hadn't had his supper yet. So he thwacked - his word -her on the bottom and said, "Is the ale cold? I crave my ale, woman." Bottom? Crave? Thwack? Woman? Utter rot. Utter rot. What kind of language is that? She had a bottom like a sieve, if you can see it, and ale only made him belch. There's a limit to everything, and they were it. Schenectady? - I never lived there, and if I did I surely don't remember it. That's a cue, no doubt. -Mal á la téte! Mal á la téte! Mal á la téte!

THE NOVELIST
by Howard Fast
Jane Austen's cottage in Chawton,
Hampshire, England, 1817
Jane Austen, the reclusive novelist, 40

Jane sickens and dies, leaving her newly found beloved, Thomas Crighton. She leaves a letter behind for him to read. *(She appears on stage to speak the words of the letter to him.)*

JANE: *(Revealed seated at writing table.)* I am not going to cry out against the fate that brought us together too late, and gave us all too little of ourselves. Whatever we had was good and wonderful, and I think more than I had ever hoped for. You chose a strange and peculiar woman indeed, a woman who could never rest on the fact that she was a woman, and could never accept the place in life that her age allocates to women. So I constructed a life, my dear Thomas, that was filled with sensible and reasonable explanations for who I was and what I was. Jane Austen, a middle-aged spinster, who whiled her time away writing entertainments that were a substitute for life. But at least I have this good fortune, that in the end I discovered a reality for which there is no substitute. It is not the length of love that matters, but rather the quality of it, and in my love for you I found a quality that was all I had ever dreamed of.

I hope that you will not move away from this place, since it is a good place and one that we came to enjoy together. If your wanderlust is indeed satisfied, then you must do the things that we had planned to do. You must find a wife for yourself who is sensible and good natured, and she should be young enough to bear your children, for you are filled with a great capacity to love and it would be sinful indeed if my own passing away were to destroy it. I have little to leave you except this - my own sense of the wonder and joy of life. You must not let that go to waste. And if you choose to think of me in the future, it must be a happy fulfilled man who thinks of the Jane Austen he once knew.

JANE [and **CRIGHTON**]: *(Together.)* "Dearly beloved, I bid you goodbye."

ONE THING IS NOT ANOTHER (A VAUDEVILLE)
by Kenneth Bernard
Here and Now
Old Woman, an old woman in a wheelchair, 60+

Here, an old woman shares a memory of her legs and a school friend.

OLD WOMAN: You wouldn't think a girl of twelve could do much wrong. And in fact I didn't. But I had this little habit of hiking up my skirt when I sat. And for a long time no one said anything. But one day Maggie noticed the stick legs were gone and my garters pinched a nice bit of flesh. She still didn't say anything, but I could see her looking and I knew what she was looking at and why, and it gave me goose pimples to know it all. It was when I didn't do any different for visiters that she decided she had to speak. "I think we should take down your hems a bit," she said the first time. But hiking is hiking, and I was thrilled by the look of my thighs, and I knew what they could do to any men that came by. Hems or not, my garters showed. One day she came right out with it. "Molly," she said, "you've got a nice woman's bit of leg there, but you're still a girl and I think I ought to tell you something." Well, she did, all right, but I knew beforehand everything she was going to say. I didn't agree with her, not on your life. But with Mother being dead and Maggie loving me so much, not to mention the cooking and the cleaning and waiting up for me, I wasn't going to say so. I just kept my head down and listened, blushing a bit at it all. She had my number, all right. But I figured I could pull my skirts down a bit for a while, at least till I was done with school. Even so, it was a comfort to me to know what I had there, covered up, and I often squeezed hard and smiled privately. But she never spoke to me about that.

IT'S RALPH

by Hugh Whitemore
A country cottage, England, the Present
Clare, a hard-working executive, 40

Clare has shared some wine with Ralph, an idealistic old friend of
her husband's. Here, she tells Ralph of her desire to believe in
God.

CLARE: Somebody once tried to prove to me that God exists.
It was a doctor. I was feeling terribly precarious. It was horrid.
I remember reading that book by Sylvia Plath, The Bell Jar, and
thinking, well that's it, that's me, I'm like her, I'm going mad. So
I went and saw a doctor. This was all years ago. It was a lady
doctor. She lived in Maida Vale, near the canal. She was very
nice, very helpful. I suppose I was expecting some sort of
explanation, some sort of answer, but of course there wasn't one,
there never is, I suppose, or rarely. *(Pause.)* I kept asking
myself unanswerable questions. Why was I born good-looking
and not ugly? Why were my parents wealthy and not poor?
Why wasn't I a starving Cambodian peasant? Why wasn't I
dying of cancer? The doctor laughed, she had a very jolly
laugh. She said I was responsible for none of these things.
"Who is?" I asked. "Nobody," she said, "God, perhaps." "I
don't believe in God," I said. "That's a pity," she said, "because
if you did you could blame Him. Wouldn't that be wonderfully
convenient?" Then she told me how you can prove that God
exists. *(She pauses for a moment, recalling the complicated
proof.)* First of all you have to define what you mean by God.
One definition is to say that God is the greatest possible being.
Someone or something that is more powerful, more creative,
and has more goodness than anyone or anything we can
imagine. God is the greatest possible being. Even if you don't
believe in God that seems a pretty reasonable definition of the
something you don't believe in. Then my doctor said to me,
"You don't believe in God but can you accept that definition of
Him?" And I said yes. Then she said, "As far as you're
concerned, God exists only in the mind and not in reality. He
certainly exists in the mind because you're thinking of Him now
and that's what it means to exist in the mind. But if God only
existed in the mind and not in reality, then you could imagine
something like the God you are thinking of in your mind but

existing in reality and therefore greater. But how can that be? You've just agreed that God is the greatest possible being and now you've imagined something greater." Even I could see that was impossible. It's a self-contradiction. Where did I go wrong? My doctor said, "The mistake was to say that God existed only in the mind. He must exist in reality as well." *(Pause.)* I was terribly impressed by that. I knew there must be a flaw in it somewhere, but I couldn't see where. I still can't. *(Pause.)* I want God to exist. I want everything to be the way I thought it was when I was a child. Then I'd be happy. Or so I like to think. *(Pause.)* Please kiss me. *(Ralph kisses her gently.)*

THE RESURRECTION OF DARK SOLDIERS
by *William Electric Black*
An apartment in New York City, the Present
Makeeba Parks, a strong advocate of civil rights,
African-American, 40's

When her husband wonders why their son has turned against their on-going struggle for civil rights, Makeeba tempers his frustration with the following explanation.

MAKEEBA: But he does, I tell you! You just shoved it down his throat until it made him turn against you. I should have stopped it sooner, but I felt it was not my place. *(Pause.)* When I was a little girl my mother made me take piano lessons. Everyday I had to sit at that piano with old Mrs. Samuels. And then for two more house I had to go over what she taught me while my mother stood by watching. She wanted so badly for me to become a great colored pianist. You were labelled colored when my mother was a child. And you had to become great in order to get that colored off your back. *(Pause.)* Well...one day I just couldn't take it anymore. Other little girls were outside playing games and sharing peppermint sticks. I began to smash that piano. First with my fist, then a lamp, then a piano stool...I went crazy as my mother ran out of the room for her life. *(Pause.)* And then you know what happened? I walked outside into the fresh air and sunshine and finally...finally I felt alive. And buck-toothed Linda Greene handed me a piece of her peppermint stick. And I smiled...and smiled.

THE RESURRECTION OF DARK SOLDIERS
by William Electric Black
An apartment in New York City, the Present
Janet Wilson, Mayor's daughther, 20

Janet recalls her kidnapping at the hands of black radical Batu
Parks to his son Zakeen Parks.

JANET: Should I fight him...let him do it. My God...I was so
terrified as I curled up on the floor of the van, bouncing to the
vibrations of the City streets. *(Pause.)* Then it all seemed like
some dream. Some twisted dream that I couldn't awake from.
(Pause.) WAKE UP, JANET! Wake up I kept saying to myself.
Did you fall asleep in the library while working on your psych
paper. GOD IT'S HOT! I can't breathe. Please wake up.
WAKE UP! *(Pause.)* And then I felt someone at my feet. He
unties me. Where am I? Am I still in the City...in the country,
still in my dream. Is the rape about to begin? *(Pause.)*
Perhaps I'm dead. Yes...that's it. This is death and for some
reason I've died and gone to Hell. *(Pause.)* Now I'm being
hustled along. A few steps...I stumble. He yells, KEEP
MOVING! I feel a gun in my ribs. The ground sounds
different. I'm inside of a building. This building. I go up in
an elevator. Up to heaven, I hope. I pray. (Pause.) It stops. I
expect all my college friends to yell surprise, but it's not my
birthday. And then I hear...WHO IS IT? IT'S ROGER, MAN!
OPEN UP THE GODDAMNED DOOR!!! *(Pause.)* I'm pulled
inside. Then more voices...tension, the smell of liquor, a voice
of authority. The voice of Batu Parks. *(Stage lights begin to
fade.)*

SERVY -N- BERNICE 4EVER
by Seth Zvi Rosenfeld
A studio apartment in Back Bay, Boston, the Present
Bernice, a beautiful young model, African-American, 20's

When Bernice's life takes a few bad turns, she calls Servy, Her
one-time lover and asks him to come for a visit. Here, she tells
him a bittersweet tale of her father.

BERNICE: *(Takes picture of her father and stares at it.)* He
was so proud that I had a scholarship to go to college that on
my eighteenth birthday, one week before I left to go to college
my father took me to Tiffany's. He wanted me to have
something to remember him by. I said, "Daddy I know you
don't have money to buy something expensive." He told me to
pick out anything I wanted. I picked out the least expensive
ring I could find. It was a thin gold ring with tiny chips of
diamonds and rubies. I showed ito to my father, he loved it, we
walked right up to the counter just as proud as could be because
he was my daddy and I was his baby and we were having this
moment, right. Now the salesman at the counter was nervous
because my father looked like a dope fiend and he knew damn
well that he wasn't suppose to be in no Tiffany's buyin' no ring
for his daughter's birthday. He says, "Is this cash or charge?"
My father gave him his credit card. The salesman took the card
and was gone a long time, my father was sweating, the man
came back with the security guard and they took my father
away...Next time I saw him I was wearing black and he was the
man in the pine box.

A SLIP OF THE TONGUE
by Dusty Hughes
A flat in Eastern Europe, the Present
Katya, a woman concerned with the state
of her country, 20-30

When her lover, a formerly censured dissident writer, questions her involvement with the new organization of Eastern Europe, Katya offers the following explanation.

KATYA: Do you know why I've joined, as you put it? Before I met you I had an affair with one of my tutors. Gornik. He was quite nice looking but he was a slob and he was married. It wasn't really an affair it was a fling. Two or three flings. He was quite charming we used to get drunk together after lectures and go to Art galleries but I got bored with him. Anyway he was unhappy with his wife etcetera etcetera. She was the daughter of someone high up in the party. She loved him. Oh, it's all so sordid. Anyway I stopped seeing him. I was going out with a guy at the film school. Gornik got really obsessed. Used to keep turning up at places unexpectedly. I tried to talk it out with him, you know it was the only way. We sat in the cafe at the station. He'd cut himself shaving and was sweating. I told him to be reasonable. I tried not to destroy his ego but I probably failed. That night he broke into my apartment and tried to rape me. I screamed the place down. The police came but I suppose his wife talked to someone because they didn't do anything. They ended up threatening me. And I had to carry on going to his tutorials. It was terrible. He even made little jokes at my expense. I wasn't his best student but I couldn't have failed those exams. I was the only one out of my year and they threw me out. My father was so proud of me I didn't know how to tell him. So I didn't. I took to hanging around the University. I couldn't keep away. And all my friends supported me. I don't know how long it would have gone on. Then things began to happen. Nobody went to classes any more. We were all out in the streets. I knew what I was doing there. It was my justice. And justice for all the ones like me who might come after. So it would never happen again. I don't want to hear about the ifs and buts, Dominic, and all the reasons in your head that tell you things are never perfect. I'm standing in the middle of events and as long as they keep happening I'm going to try and control them.

SPIKE HEELS
by Theresa Rebeck
Boston, the Present
Georgie, late 20's

Georgie is frustrated by her new secretarial job and is riding the subway home. She reveals her frustration to her friend Andrew.

GEORGIE: I wish I still smoked. Why the hell did I have to quit smoking? I loved smoking. Do you have any cigarettes? How the hell are we supposed to survive in this stupid country without cigarettes? I mean, they invent this terrific little antidote to everything, cigarettes, and then after they get you hooked on it they tell you that it's going to kill you. And you know, the thing is, I think I'd rather be killed by cancer than by life in general. I really think that.

SPIKE HEELS

by Theresa Rebeck

Boston, the Present

Georgie, late 20's

Georgie has admitted to throwing a pencil at her boss to her
friend, Andrew. Andrew suggests she couldn't hold a job at
McDonald's with such behavior. Georgie responds.

GEORGIE: *(Ignoring him overlapping.)* Jesus, I was a
goddam waitress for seven years, the customers fucking loved
me. You think I talk like this in front of strangers; you think I
don't have a brain in my head or something? That is so fucking
condescending. Anytime I lose my temper, I'm crazy, is that it?
You dont just make these assumptions. Well, fuck you, Andrew.
I mean it. Fuck you. *(She takes her clothes in her hands and
heads for the door.)*

[**ANDREW:** You can't go out in the hall like that--]

GEORGIE: I mean, I just love that. You don't even know.
You've never seen me in that office. You think I'm, like,
incapable of acting like somebody I'm not? For four months
I've been scared to death but I do it, you know, I take messages,
I call the court, I write his damn letters. I watch my mouth, I
dress like this--whatever this is; these are the ugliest clothes I
have ever seen--I am gracious, I am bright, I am promising. I
am being this other person for them because I do want this job
but there is a point beyond which I will not be fucked with! So
you finally push me beyond that point, and I throw the pencil
and now you're going to tell me that that is my problem? What,
do you guys think you hold all the cards or something? You
think you have the last word on reality? You do, you think that
anything you do to me is okay as long as it's phrased properly,
and anything I do is fucked because I'm not using the right
words. I'm, like, throwing pencils and saying fuck you, I'm
speaking another language, that's my problem. And the thing
is--I am America. You know? You guys are not America. You
think you are; Jesus Christ, you guys think you own the world.
It's like, you guys think you can say anything you want if you
phrase it right and look good while you say it! I mean, who
made up that rule, Andrew? And do you actually think we're
buying it? *(Pause.)*

SPILT MILK
by *Glenn Alterman*
New York City, Present
Edna, 60's

Murry asks Edna how her sister is when she returns from a hospital visit.

EDNA: *(Turning around to him)* How is she?! What kina...?! *(She stops herself)* Don't ask. The same. Same as always. Same as yesterday, day before. Jus' stares up at the ceilin'. Lies there in that hospital an' talks...talks ta ah don't know who. Angels on the ceilin' a somethin. Who the hell knows who she talks to anymore. Who can understand her? Maybe she's preparin', Murry. Gettin' ready to go. Who knows? She jus' talks an' talks in like baby talk. A conversation - ta nobody. Thin air.

[**MURRAY:** Hm. Shame. She know ya taday?]

EDNA: Nah. She don't know nobody no more. She jus'...I don't know. But ahl tell ya Murry. There was a second taday. Jus' a second, where from the corner of her eye, I saw like a glimmer, y'know? She gay me a look. An' was like ole times. *(She smiles.)* An' I remembered that look from way back when. Fa' jus' one moment Murry, I thought maybe she's gonna snap out of it. Maybe a miracle! Say "I was jus' pretendin', Edna. Foolin' aroun'. S'gonna be okay again. Jus' like ole times." An' she'd throw the blankets back, y'know, jump outta bed, an' say, "Come on! Come Edna, let's go shoppin'!" An we'd grab our bags an' run downtown like we usta. But...was jus' a look. Meant nothin'. Nothin' at all.

STORIES FROM THE NATIONAL ENQUIRER
by Jeanne Murray Walker
Remers, Minnesota
Liz, 30's, former actress turned waitress

Liz tells Leonard about her daughter and about beauty

LIZ: (*Silence, then slowly*) It's her lip, her face, the whole side of her face (*Pause.*) I heard some junior high school boys call her a monster, once.

[**LEONARD:** What does she look like?]

LIZ: (*Torn, reluctantly*) She has long, blond shiny hair, I braid it in the mornings. I touch it. It's soft. (*Long pause.*) I've saved my beauty against the name they call her. Monster. (Pause.) A long time ago, I gave up caring about beauty -- As if it were a rhinestone button on my coat and one day it grew wobbly. One thread gave up and then one more, until the button was hanging off the coat. Finally, I ripped it free.

[**L E O N A R D :** I don't understand.] (*Leonard forgets his notebook. He watches Liz with rapt attention.*)

LIZ: I can still feel beauty when I want to, small and hard as a button in my pocket underneath my finger tips. I's like to give it to her. May it be all the looks she'll ever need, my face fixed in magazines and films -- My face is like a mask that traps me. But now, with her here, her face off center, barely but terribly wrong, I see how to escape.

[**LEONARD:** Escape?]

LIZ: I'll go with her as she makes her way from that fixed beauty, as the milky way spins from earth, like flock on flock of buttons, cut loose together, spiraling upward, opening out to everything imperfect, deep and promising. I want to learn to spin away from those old finished pictures of myself, to wheel into the darkness where she is, breathing further and further out, passing winking stars that no astronomer has thought of, till I get to the last, brightest star, which is her face. (*Leonard* *reaches out and touches Liz. Coming to her senses)* That's my story. *(Bitterly)* <u>Beauty Queen Has Monster Baby</u>. Now you can make a fool of me, too.

STORIES FROM THE NATIONAL ENQUIRER
by Jeanne Murray Walker
Remers, Minnesota
Rosalee, 50's, a woman who is possessed by angels

Rosalee tells Leonard, a National Enquirer reporter about her angels.

ROSALEE: Well, he lied to me, that doctor from the state. When I saw him through the keyhole coming for me, a hundred angels climbed down my back, rung by rung to my knees and hid their faces. "This will not hurt you," he promised, and laced me into a straight jacket. He pushed me out into a fever. In that noon glare I was the only one who couldn't move. I couldn't move. I couldn't save my angels. So they flew past my hand, which was pinned open by by side. Smelling like rhubarb, their wings stabbing sunshine like umbrellas, they broke from me. I was the one left naked, all of my dark joy gone. Thanslucent as a fish whose guts have been scraped out, the skin ripped off, the bones sliced out, a fish whose body finally lies so luminous you can see through it. I was invisible. I learned to talk. After several months they brought me home. At first I stood right here at the cracked window, trying to recall them, trying to turn that gray stone by the sidewalk back into angels. Trying to make an angel of the dog tied on the porch across the street where the Cronin boys notched my bones to make a ladder for their feet. But they didn't know how to come. Poor wings were lost.

[**LEONARD:** (*Very shaken*) Mrs. Truax?]

ROSALEE: Yes, sir?

[**LEONARD:** Thank you.]

ROSALEE: I also know a story about Ezekiel and wheels within wheels.

[**LEONARD:** (*Getting up to leave*) That's all right. This is all I need.]

ROSALEE: Jesus go with you, Mr. Milgram If you see any of my lost angels, send them home.

TRUST

by Steven Dietz
New York City, Present
Gretchen, 35

Gretchen, a dressmaker, tells Becca, who she is fitting, a story of infatuation.

GRETCHEN: It was before she was well known. She was singing a lot of bars, bowling alleys, private parties. She'd have eight or nine gigs a week. It was tearing her voice to shreds.

She went to a voice specialist -- she was completely hoarse at this point -- and the specialist said she had nodes on her vocal chords and that she had one of two choices: she could have surgery to have them removed, which didn't guarantee that she'd ever get her voice back; or, she could remain silent -- completely silent -- for three months. In three months, he said, the vocal chords would heal themselves.

We were roommates. We had a one - bedroom on Franklin. I had the bedroom. She had the hide - a - bed. Tiny place. Lots of macaroni and votive candles in stolen ashtrays.

Leah decided not to speak for three months.

We developed a plan. We went to K-mart and bought a bunch of those plastic erasable notepads.

[**BECCA:** Like when you're a kid.]

GRETCHEN: And you yank the plastic sheet back and the pad is empty again.

[**BECCA:** Right.]

GRETCHEN: We put them all over the apartment, in the bathroom, we put one in the car, we carried them in our purses. We had them everywhere.

And for three months, Leah wrote me every single word she wanted to say. I spoke for her on the phone, I spoke for her in

73

public. We spent every minute together.

And, at first, it was stuff like "I'm hungry. Let's get a pizza." Or "I thought you paid the phone bill." But as days went by, she got more comfortable with it. With me. And, as she got more comfortable, she censored less. She let herself think out - loud onto that little plastic pad. We'd sit and drink wine till sun - up, me talking, she writing by the light of some bayberry candle.

It went on from there. She started letting me read everything. Not just her conversation, but her letters, her lyrics, her diary, everything. It seemed perfectly natural. It was who we were then. It was rope connecting us.

I gave over to it. And I lost sight of who was who. Where did she begin? Where did I stop?

Of course, the day she was hoping for was the day I was dreading. And, three months later, it came. Her voice was back. Tentative, at first, but within a few weeks she was singing again. Her new songs caught the eye of a small label who sold her stuff to a big label and off she went.

I denied everything to myself, of course. She's your *friend*. That's *it*. You helped her through a hard time. Of *course* you miss the time you had together. It was *constant*. it was *charged*. Of *course* it can't be like that anymore.

So, I resented her. Not just occasionally. *Every time she talked*. Especially to other people, on the phone, at the grocery store, anywhere. I wanted her back.

[BECCA: But you didn't tell her.]

GRETCHEN: Of course I didn't tell her. I just treated her like shit. Because, hey, you know how these things work, because *I loved her.*

One morning I was sitting in a chair, staring out the window. And I realized that I couldn't for the life of me remember when it had been lovely.

So, I wrote her a note on one of those K-mart pads. And I left.

And after that, whenever I was curious about her, all I had to do was read People magazine. (*Silence.*)

[BECCA: (*Gently.*) You miss her.]

GRETCHEN: I don't miss her. I miss how I felt with her. There's a difference.

TRAVELS WITH MY AUNT
by Graham Greene
Adapted for the stage by Giles Havergal
A flat in London
Aunt Augusta, an outspoken and lively senior citizen, 60-70

Following her sister's cremation, Augusta shares a gruesome yet
fascinating anecdote with her nephew.

AUNT AUGUSTA: I can say now to both of you how relieved
I am that everything this afternoon went without a hitch. I once
attended a very important funeral - the wife of a famous man of
letters who had not been the most faithful of husbands. It was
soon after the first great war. I was very interested at that time
in the Fabians. I arrived early as a spectator and I was leaning
ove the Communion rail - trying to make out the names on the
wreaths - and I must have accidentally touched a button. The
coffin began to slide away, the doors opened, I could feel the
hot air of the oven and hear the flap of the flames, the coffin
went in and the doors closed, and at that very moment in walked
the whole grand party, Mr. and Mrs. Bernard Shaw, Mr H.G.
Wells, Doctor Havelock Ellis, Mr. Ramsay MacDonald, and the
widower. The clergyman *(non-denominational of course)* led
us in the humanist hymn "Cosmos, O Cosmos, Cosmos shall we
call Thee?" I buried my face in my handkerchief and simulated
grief, but you know I don't think anyone (except, I suppose, the
clergyman and he kept dumb about it) noticed that the coffin
wasn't there. The widower certainly didn't, but then he hadn't
noticed his wife for some years. Doctor Havelock Ellis made a
very moving address *(or so it seemed to me then; I hadn't finally
plumped for Catholicism, though I was on the brink)* about the
dignity of a funeral service conducted without illusions or
rhetoric. He could truthfully have said without a corpse too.
Everybody was quite satisfied.

UNIDENTIFIED HUMAN REMAINS
AND THE TRUE NATURE OF LOVE
by Brad Fraser
Edmonton, Alberta, 1988
Benita, a woman with a preoccupation
with the macabre, 30's

A woman of alleged psychic abilities, Benita here muses on a gruesome yet familiar folktale.

BENITA: What about this one? This guy and his girlfriend are parked in a lovers lane necking when a special report comes on the radio and says that there's an escaped killer in the neighbourhood and everyone should stay inside and lock their doors and windows because the guy's crazy and he's got a hook where one of his hands used to be.

Well of course the girl's real scared and wants to leave right away, but the guy's got a bone on and doesn't want to stop until the girl gets good and mad and says if he won't drive her home she'll get out and walk.

So he gets pissed off and slams the car into gear and tears off, real abrupt, calling the girl a chicken and all that. When they get to her place he hops out of the car and goes around to open her door for her.

Then all of a sudden this big guy screams, turns white and faints. The girl thinks "What the hell?" and gets out. When she closes the door she sees a bloody hook hanging from the door handle. *(She laughs.)* That's a good one.

UNPUBLISHED LETTERS
by Jonathan C. Levine
An apartment in New York, the Present
Carol, a woman coping with the death of her father, 30's

Carol has led a quiet life in a rural area. When her father, a well-known writer, dies, she travels to New York City for his funeral. There, she meets her half brother for the first time and decides to move in with him. Here she describes her life at home.

CAROL: I didn't have to come to New York. My life is all right the way it is. I have a good job I like enough. At five o'clock I leave and go to the diner. Everyone there is friendly to me. They all remember me as the smart fat girl sitting at the back table doing her homework. Diners are very nice places to be. You probably didn't know that. You probably think they're places to stay away from. But, a diner is the best place to go if you want a home-cooked meal, and you have no home. You can get a complete dinner in a diner. That's bread and butter. Soup and salad. Entree with potatoes and vegetables. Dessert and coffee. And if it's the frank and beans entree or the meatloaf with brown gravy, you get all that for $3.95. That's a fair price for all that. But you see, if you do have a home, or if you have a family or if you want something a little more than a home-cooked meal and the local talk, then you gotta leave the diner. You owe it to yourself to pack your bags and leave and hope you'll be all right somewhere else. I feel bad that I chose you to come to, 'cause you're not happy and you don't feel like being nice to anyone else. But my next best choice was your brother. And I think that the first thing a person should do when they get up enough courage to make their life a little better and leave Corlstown, is not to rush off to Kenya. if you really don't want me to stay, I'm not going to. I'll leave. I'll just have to be braver than I thought I'd have to be.

THE VISIT
by Friedrich Duerrenmatt
Adapted by Maurice Valency
A small town in Central Europe, 1950's
Claire, an incredibly wealthy woman seeking justice, 50's

Claire has returned to the small town of her youth with the sole purpose of punishing the man who disgraced her so many years ago. Here, she confronts her one-time lover.

CLAIRE: How strange it is, Anton! How clearly it comes back to me! The day we saw one another for the first time, do you remember - I was on a balcony then. It was a day like today, a day in autumn without a breath of wind, warm as it is now - only lately I am always cold. You stood down there and stared at me without moving. I was embarrassed. I didn't know what to do. I wanted to go back into the darkness of the room where it was safe, but I couldn't. You stared up at me darkly, almost angrily, as if you wished to hurt me, but your eyes were full of passion. *(Schill begins to lower the gun, involuntarily.)* Then, I don't know why, I left the balcony and I came down and stood in the street beside you. You didn't greet me, you didn't say a word, but you took my hand and we walked together out of the town into the fields, and behind us came Kobby and Lobby, like two dogs, snivelling and giggling and snarling. Suddenly you picked up a stone and hurled it at them, and they ran yelping back into the town, and we were alone. *(Schill has lowered the rifle completely. He moves forward toward her as close as he can come.)* That was the beginning and everything else had to follow. There is no escape.

WINCHELSEA DROUND AND OTHER PLAYS
by Don Nigro
Here and Now
Madeline, a young woman who likes the dark, 25

Here, a young woman tells a pleasingly erotic tale about an encounter with a rainstorm.

MADELINE: There's something about riding the bus at night, moving through the darkness on a cold or rainy night, the way the dark surrounds you and overwhelms you and the illusion of safety you have there in your seat by the window with the sleeping people all around you, all the lights turned off, not knowing if the driver is awake or not. It's eerie, and wonderful, and vaguely sexual. In winter, seeing the Christmas decorations of isolated houses going by in the dark, Dickensian, safe, dangerous, but nestled in the precious illusion of safety. My favorite place, almost. Maybe it reminds me of when I was a very small child and we'd be driving home at night from somebody's house and I would curl up in the little carpeted well on the floor of the back seat of my father's new car, curl myself up like a cat, and the night would be all around us, and the road would be going by underneath me and I'd feel as safe and secure as if I was in the womb again. There's something so comforting and unreal about the darkness, I mean, the real darkness of small towns, and villages and farms and countryside and woods at night, not the darkness of cities, but the ancient dark, the dark we come from when we're born, and go to when we die. The darkness of God.

THE WINTER WIFE

by Claire Tomalin

A holiday villa in Menton on the French Rivera, 1920
Katherine Mansfield, a writer of short fiction, 31

In the final years of her life, tuberculosis has brought Katherine to
Menton in search of a cure. Here, she confronts her doctor with
the fact of his own illness.

KATHERINE: Dr. Bouchage, I told you that I am a writer. I
have, on your advice, given up the work I was doing for my
husband's magazine. That doesn't matter. But now I have to
write for myself. You understand what I mean? You have seen
me over these months at Menton. You know something about
me - something of my temperament, something of my history;
some of the bad things that have happened to me. I have things
I want to write. If I do not have long to live, I want to spend the
time I have in saying - or in starting to say - what I know about
the world. About men and women. About human indifference
and cruelty and stupidity. About the way in which people
devour one another, and poison one another. About the
importance of hate. *(Pause.)* There are so many things I want
to describe! What it is like to be an ordinary, healthy woman -
Marie, say, going to the market under the green and gold shade
of the plane trees, through streets that smell of lemons and fresh
coffee - past cafés where lovers who imagine they are happy are
sitting under the pink and white umbrellas - past the fountain
where she stops to talk to other ordinary, healthy women with
their water pots - feeling on their faces and arms the warm wind
off the sea. The treacherous sea. All this, all this: and to know
in your own bones nothing but suffering and death. *(Pause.
Bouchage is looking at her intently, and listening.)* And you,
Doctor Bouchage: you know very well what I mean, I believe.
All this time you have been plumbing my depths, finding out
my secrets, I have been observing you too, and finding out
yours. You may be the doctor, but I am the writer. And just as
you can tell things about myself, I can tell you something about
myself, I can tell you something about yourself. You know that
my life is burning away - more or less quickly -but I know that
you are also touched by the same burning frost. *(Bouchage,
who has been listening intently, is extremely disconcerted, and
holds up his hand, but she continues.)* I can see it in your eyes

81

and feel it when you touch me with your good, sensitive fingers. you are too quick, too kind, too responsive, too eager. If you are a good doctor, it is because you are almost as sick as I am.

[BOUCHAGE: You are an observant woman, Mrs. Murry, as well as a gifted one.]

KATHERINE: And are you going north, Doctor Bouchage? Which mountains are you going to settle in? Or are you going to stay here with Madame Bouchage and your little son, in the treacherous bright sunshine, beside the treacherous bright sea, for as long as the burning frost allows you? Enjoying your life and your work, in the company of the people you love best, for as long as the gods permit?

(*Bouchage is now looking down and will not raise his eyes to meet those of Katherine.*)

I recognise you, and you recognise me, because we are the same, Dr. Bouchage. We have both been corruped by something bad. Consumption - tuberculosis - whatever name it bears. And neither of us is likely to escape from the bad things that have entered into us. But I'll do as you say. I'll go to Switzerland with Miss Baker, and I'll let her look after me. I'll take your letter humbly and gratefully, in which you pass on to another doctor all the things you have found out about my illnesses - my disgraceful scars and symptoms, all the sins of my youth laid bare.

One thing I shall not promise you, though. (*Now Bouchage looks up.*) I do not intend to give up my work. On the contrary, I intend from now on to work harder than I have ever worked in my life.

THE WINTER WIFE
by Claire Tomalin
A holiday villa in Menton on the French Rivera, 1920
Katherine Mansfield, a writer of short fiction, 31

Katherine has just completed a short story, and in the happy flush of success has managed to put her illness at bay for a moment or two. Here, she shares memories from the past with her faithful companion, Ida.

KATHERINE: Bliss. This reminds me of school. Feasts in bed. No grown man ever appreciates how good food tastes in bed. But can we ever have been fifteen, Ida? Just think, girls of fifteen, how perfect they can be - just budding, so eager, so avid for everything. So pleased with themselves. With such appetites. With this great expanse of time in front of them.

[IDA: You had a nightdress with tiny yellow flowers all over it. And a blue silk dressing gown from Marshall & Snelgrove.]

KATHERINE: But it's better than those old times at college now, though, don't you think? I mean, we are really ourselves now, aren't we? Listen, Ida. We must be happy together now. No more blackness from me. No more - silliness from you. You can be very, very silly. But there are to be no more makeshifts, no failures from now on. I'm writing - I'm writing well. No reason why we shouldn't be happy. Perhaps I shall spare six months a year for Jack *(Her eye lights on the photograph.)* - to keep him happy - because I do love him in spite of all - and six with you -and we'll share everything. Let's see: we'll have tea in forest glades, and go swimming in - Corsica, why not Corsica, don't you long to go there? In the afternoons, we'll attend concerts in public gardens. We'll have picnics on rocks by the sea - anything we have a fancy to do - and I'll work and work, and earn money for us. And I'll be famous - scandalously famous. You'll see.